# 50 WALKS IN

# Warwickshire & West Midlands

## 50 WALKS OF 2–10 MILES

First published 2003
New edition 2009
Reprinted February and July 2010

Researched and written by Andrew Noyce
Field checked and updated 2009
by Martin Andrew

Commissioning Editor: Sandy Draper
Senior Editors: David Popey
and Penny Fowler
Designer: Tracey Butler
Picture Research: Vivien Little
Proofreader: Sandy Draper
Cartography provided by the Mapping
Services Department of AA Publishing

Produced by AA Publishing
© AA Media Limited 2010

Published by AA Publishing (a trading name
of AA Media Limited, whose registered office
is Fanum House, Basing View, Basingstoke,
Hampshire RG21 4EA; registered number
06112600)

  This product includes
mapping data licensed
from the Ordnance Survey® with the
permission of the Controller of Her
Majesty's Stationery Office. © Crown
Copyright 2010. All rights reserved.
Licence number 100021153.

A04520

ISBN: 978-0-7495-6295-3
ISBN: 978-0-7495-6328-8 (SS)

A CIP catalogue record for this book is
available from the British Library.

The contents of this book are believed
correct at the time of printing. Nevertheless,
the publishers cannot be held responsible
for any errors or omissions or for changes
in the details given in this book or for
the consequences of any reliance on the
information it provides. This does not affect
your statutory rights. We have tried to
ensure accuracy in this book, but things do
change and we would be grateful if readers
would advise us of any inaccuracies they
may encounter.

We have taken all reasonable steps to
ensure that these walks are safe and
achievable by walkers with a realistic level
of fitness. However, all outdoor activities
involve a degree of risk and the publishers
accept no responsibility for any injuries
caused to readers whilst following these
walks. For more advice on walking safely
see page 144. The mileage range shown
on the front cover is for guidance only
— some walks may be less than or exceed
these distances.

Some of the walks may appear in other AA
books and publications.

Visit AA Publishing at theAA.com/shop

Cover reproduction by Keenes
Group, Andover
Printed by Printer Trento Srl, Italy

Acknowledgements
The Automobile Association wishes to
thank the following photographers and
organisations for their assistance in the
preparation of this book.

Abbreviations for the picture credits are as
follows — (AA) AA World Travel Library

3 AA/C Jones; 9 AA/C Jones; 34/35 AA/C
Jones; 42/43 AA/C Jones; 68 AA/C Jones; 73
AA/H Palmer; 82/83 AA/C Jones; 94 AA/C
Jones; 100 AA/C Jones; 116/117 AA/C Jones;
124 AA/C Jones; 128 AA/C Jones

Illustrations by Andrew Hutchinson

Every effort has been made to trace the
copyright holders, and we apologise in
advance for any accidental errors. We would
be happy to apply any corrections in the
following edition of this publication.

*Right: A frosty path on Wychbury Hill in Pedmore (Walk 2)*

# 50 WALKS IN
# Warwickshire & West Midlands

## 50 WALKS OF 2–10 MILES

# Contents

# Contents

## Rating

Each walk is rated for its relative difficulty compared to the other walks in this book. Walks marked +++ are likely to be shorter and easier with little total ascent. The hardest walks are marked +++

## Walking in Safety

For advice and safety tips see page 144.

# Locator Map

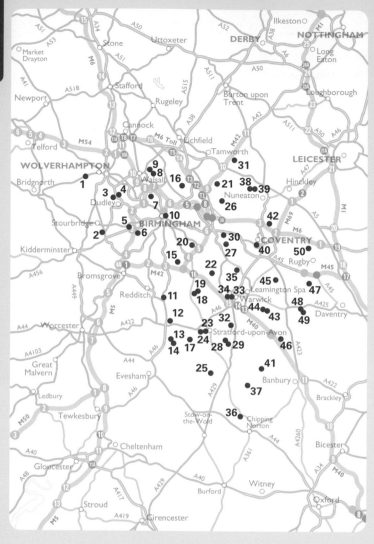

# Legend

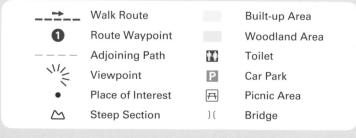

| | | | |
|---|---|---|---|
| ⇢ —— Walk Route | | Built-up Area | |
| ❶ Route Waypoint | | Woodland Area | |
| — — — Adjoining Path | | 🚻 Toilet | |
| ⚊ Viewpoint | | P Car Park | |
| ● Place of Interest | | 🚏 Picnic Area | |
| △ Steep Section | | )( Bridge | |

# Introducing Warwickshire & West Midlands

The sparkle of early morning sunlight on a country river as it meanders through beautiful countryside; the reflections of sailing boats on a country lake; relaxing with a pint in the garden of an old English pub in a picturesque village; the sight of colourful narrow boats making their way through a flight of lock gates; the visual impact created by an historic castle. These are just a few of the experiences that can be enjoyed in Warwickshire and the West Midlands. These two counties form the picturesque and historic Heart of England and an ancient cross in the village of Meriden supposedly marks the spot regarded as the very centre of England. There may be few seriously high hills in this fertile plain, but it is an area full of attractive walking in rolling countryside, blessed with a fascinating history and many wonderful places and buildings to visit.

Warwickshire is Shakespeare's county and the footprint of the famous Bard appears almost everywhere. The West Midlands is dominated by the great industrial city of Birmingham and embraces the Black Country whose limitless energy has helped shape the destiny of Britain.

William Shakespeare is probably the most famous playwright the world has known. Born and brought up around the beautiful Warwickshire town of Stratford-upon-Avon, many of his plays draw upon his own experiences in the area. In his youth, Stratford was an important market town and this gave him the opportunity to note the manners, dress and speech of the tradesmen, farmers, milkmaids, lawyers and others who attended on market day. Stratford was a centre of government and rural business matters, with one of the finest grammar schools in the country. Today, the swans gather by Clopton Bridge to be fed by the tourists who come to visit the home of the Bard.

Warwickshire has a history that embraces the Civil War, and many castles and large country houses are scattered over the county. Warwick Castle is the home of the Earl of Warwick; Kenilworth Castle was a stronghold for lords and kings of England in the 11th and 12th centuries; Ragley Hall is the home of Lord Hertford; Coughton Court is the home of the Throckmorton family and history connects it with the Gunpowder Plot; Baddesley Clinton Manor House contains a number of priest's holes to hide the clergy from Cromwell's men; Packwood House has a garden of yew trees that represent Christ, the four

## PUBLIC TRANSPORT

Either the start points of the walks or the villages en route are within easy reach from public transport. Walks 2, 3, 4, 10, 15, 16, 18, 19, 20, 23, 24, 31, 33, 34, 40 and 42 all start close to railway stations. For train times call the 24-hour national train information line 08457 48 49 50 or go online to www. nationalrail.co.uk. For times of buses and leaflets/maps of public transport routes call Traveline 0871 200 22 33. Their website (www.traveline.org.uk) has maps with a list of train stations across Warwickshire and the West Midlands. Alternatively, plan your journey at www.transportdirect.info.

evangelists, the apostles and the multitude at the sermon on the mount; Upton House is a fine William and Mary mansion; Compton Wynyates is one of the most beautiful Tudor houses in the country; and Charlecote House is where Shakespeare is said to have been caught poaching deer.

The West Midlands was central to Britain's development during the Industrial Revolution. Canals were built to transport coal, ironware, glass, pottery and textiles across the country and it remains a vibrant area of business. Today, there are fine parkland areas intermixed with the urban sprawl and many historic places to visit. These walks take you on a journey through some of the fascinating places, where the Industrial Revolution developed in its early years and many of Shakespeare's haunts.

# Using this book

### Information panels

An information panel for each walk shows its relative difficulty (see Page 4), the distance and total amount of ascent. An indication of the gradients you will encounter is shown by the rating ▲ ▲ ▲ (no steep slopes) to ▲ ▲ ▲ (several very steep slopes).

### Maps

There are 30 maps, covering 40 of the walks. Some walks have a suggested option in the same area. The information panel for these walks will tell you how much extra walking is involved. On short-cut suggestions the panel will tell you the total distance if you set out from the start of the main walk. Where an option returns to the same point on the main walk, just the distance of the loop is given. Where an option leaves the main walk at one point and returns to it at another, then the distance shown is for the whole walk. The minimum time suggested is for reasonably fit walkers and doesn't allow for stops. Each walk has a suggested map.

### Start Points

The start of each walk is given as a six-figure grid reference prefixed by two letters indicating which 100km square of the National Grid it refers to. You'll find more information on grid references on most Ordnance Survey maps.

### Dogs

We have tried to give dog owners useful advice about how dog friendly each walk is. Please respect other countryside users. Keep your dog under control, especially around livestock, and obey local bylaws and other dog control notices.

### Car Parking

Many of the car parks suggested are public, but occasionally you may find you have to park on the roadside or in a lay-by. Please be considerate when you leave your car, ensuring that access roads or gates are not blocked and that other vehicles can pass safely.

*Right: A peacock in Peacock Garden in Warwick Castle, Warwick (Walk 33)*

# Along the Staffordshire & Worcestershire Canal

*An easy, family walk following the canal and a section of the disused Kingswinford railway track.*

---

**DISTANCE** 4.5 miles (7.2km)   **MINIMUM TIME** 1hr 30min

**ASCENT/GRADIENT** 59ft (18m) ▲▲▲   **LEVEL OF DIFFICULTY** ✦✦✦

**PATHS** *Canal tow path, disused railway track and field paths, 1 stile*

**LANDSCAPE** *Open countryside near urban residences*

**SUGGESTED MAP** *OS Explorer 219 Wolverhampton & Dudley*

**START/FINISH** *Grid reference: SP 869982*

**DOG FRIENDLINESS** *Off lead along tow path and disused railway, otherwise under control*

**PARKING** *Near Mermaid pub, Wightwick*

**PUBLIC TOILETS** *None on route*

---

This is a journey into the 18th and 19th centuries – a time when the canals and railways preceded our modern, noisy road network. The walk follows the tow path of the Staffordshire and Worcestershire Canal and a stretch of disused railway line to Compton. Nearby Wightwick (pronounced 'Wittick') Manor is easy to visit along the route (see While You're There).

## Canal Revolution

If a contest for the Greatest Briton had taken place at the end of the 19th century, one of the main contenders would surely have been James Brindley. He helped to revolutionise Britain's transport system by building a series of remarkable canals that linked virtually all of the major cities in Britain . The Staffordshire and Worcestershire Canal was one of his early constructions, built to link the Severn at Stourport with the Trent at Great Heywood and carry coal from the Staffordshire coalfields. Brindley's waterways were built on the contour principle, following the lie of the land. This approach avoided straight lines of canal, deep cuttings, massive embankments and large groups of lock gates. Work on the Staffordshire and Worcestershire Canal began in 1766 and was eventually completed in 1772. When you walk along the tow path you can imagine the dirty barges of the late 18th and early 19th centuries being hauled along by horses, accompanied by inquisitive children, dogs and local people. Commercial traffic finally ceased on the canal in 1960 and in 1978 the whole canal, including its buildings and its signs, was designated a conservation area.

As the Industrial Revolution progressed, steam trains effectively replaced canal barges, but there were gaps in the rail network. The Kingswinford branch was built by the Great Western Railway to fill one of these, allowing through traffic from Bridgnorth to Wolverhampton. It opened in 1925 but was never a great success for passengers. It became a freight-only line in 1932, carrying people again briefly during World War Two, when it was used to transfer wounded soldiers from the Normandy landings. The last

# WIGHTWICK

train ran in 1965. The lines were then dismantled and the Kingswinford Railway Walk was introduced to allow local people to use the former line for leisure purposes. When you walk along the now disused railway, try to visualise youngsters peering over the railway bridges through a cloud of smoke to get a glimpse of the mighty trains as they chuffed their way along the cutting.

Today pleasure boats use the canal and its tow path combines with the disused railway to provide a fine urban walk away from the noise of the busy road traffic.

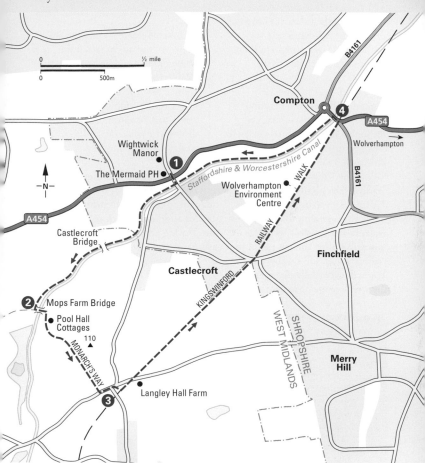

## WALK 1 DIRECTIONS

❶ From the car park, cross the A454 at the pedestrian crossing to enter Windmill Lane. Bear right and descend to the tow path of the Staffordshire and Worcestershire Canal, heading right in a south-westerly direction. After passing the Cee-Ders Club (on the far

side of the canal), you reach open countryside, with ducks, coots and moorhens for company. This stretch of the canal is similar to a river and you are likely to see anglers fishing for perch, roach, chub, bream or carp. You may even see a colourful narrowboat pass by. Continue beneath bridge No 55 (Castlecroft

*11*

# WIGHTWICK

Bridge) and along the tow path until you come to bridge No 54 (Mops Farm Bridge).

**2** Leave the tow path and cross the bridge. Go right past Pool Hall Cottages and follow the waymarkers of the Monarch's Way, heading generally south-east. At first the path is to the right of the field hedge then, later, it crosses over to the left-hand side via a stile until you come to another stile to reach Langley Road.

**3** Go left up the road and immediately past the junction bear right at the post box, go through a fence gap into the picnic area and descend steps to the dismantled railway. Head left and follow the Kingswinford (South Staffordshire) Railway Walk. This is easy walking and you are likely to meet a number of other walkers and possibly cyclists. You will follow the course of the railway for about 2 miles (3.2km). You will eventually pass beneath the road bridge near Castlecroft

### WHERE TO EAT AND DRINK

Eating out in the small front garden of The Mermaid watching the world go by is the perfect way to end a perfect day. Children are also welcome. If you visit Wightwick Manor, you can enjoy a quiet leisurely lunch in the Tea Room on Wednesdays, Thursdays and bank holidays.

via a kissing gate; following this there are moments when the scene opens up. After passing the Wolverhampton Environment Centre and the remains of Compton Station's platform you come to Compton. Leave the disused railway line and descend to the A454, going left.

**4** Cross the road, then the canal bridge to descend to the tow path, pass beneath bridge number 59 and take it back to bridge No 56, passing a couple of lock gates and a number of moored narrowboats. Go beneath bridge No 56 and leave the canal on to the pavement of Windmill Lane. Continue towards the main A454 road and cross over to return to the Mermaid in Wightwick.

### WHAT TO LOOK OUT FOR

You may not see a horse-drawn coal barge as you stroll the tow path of the 46-mile (74km) long Staffordshire and Worcestershire Canal, but you are likely to meet a colourful narrowboat making its way through one of the lock gates. Pause a while and watch how it is lifted or dropped to another level. Compton Lock, just beyond Compton village, was the first lock to be built on this canal.

### WHILE YOU'RE THERE

Nearby Wightwick Manor was built in 1887 by the Mander family. This half-timbered building is now owned and maintained by the National Trust. The influence of the 19th-century decorative artist William Morris is clear to see. Original Morris wallpapers, Pre-Raphaelite pictures, stained glass by C E Kempe and De Morgan tiles are on display. There are also fine gardens laid out with terraces and pools and some splendid yew hedges and topiary.

# Pedmore and Palladian Hagley Park

*A stroll into the country from Pedmore reveals
a magnificent view from the Obelisk.*

| | |
|---|---|
| DISTANCE 4.25 miles (6.8km) | MINIMUM TIME 2hrs |
| ASCENT/GRADIENT 279ft (85m) ▲▲▲ | LEVEL OF DIFFICULTY +++ |

PATHS *Field paths, farm tracks and roadside pavement, 6 stiles*

LANDSCAPE *Urban residential area towards Clent Hills*

SUGGESTED MAP *OS Explorer 219 Wolverhampton & Dudley*

START/FINISH *Grid reference: SP 913821*

DOG FRIENDLINESS *On lead at all times through residential areas,
off lead on Wychbury Hill*

PARKING *Roadside in Pedmore Lane, or Pedmore Hall Lane, Pedmore*

PUBLIC TOILETS *None on route*

For much of this walk there are fine views into Worcestershire over the Clent Hills, and the best of these is from the Obelisk, with Hagley Hall in the valley below. From the suburban West Midlands, town paths take you into the countryside, then link with farm tracks and the North Worcestershire Path, following part of the Monarch's Way over Wychbury Hill.

## A Stately House

Set below the range of the Clent Hills, on the outskirts of the village of Hagley, is one of the stateliest houses in England. Hagley Hall was the last of the great Palladian houses to be built. It was designed by Sanderson Miller and built between 1754 and 1760 for George, the 1st Lord Lyttelton (who was secretary to the Prince of Wales), on the site of an earlier house. The impressive building is constructed of brown stone, a rich colour that contrasts well with the Clent Hills in the background and the hall's raised lawns. Its roof balustrades, pedimented in pure Classical style, run the length of the four square-towered wings in the tradition of Inigo Jones.

## Fire and Hellfire

In 1925 a serious fire caused a great deal of damage to the interior of the building but, thankfully, it has since been restored to its former glory. The entrance hall is decorated with lovely stucco work and the dining room, one of the rooms most badly affected by the fire, has an impressive rococo ceiling. Rich tapestries and fine Van Dyke paintings are the main feature of the gallery. The 2nd Lord Lyttleton was a founder member of the infamous so-called Hellfire Club of 18th-century aristocratic libertines, along with Sir Francis Dashwood of West Wycombe. Littleton was a great gambler and on one occasion gambled the whole of Hagley Hall against a single painting. Luckily he won the bet and kept his home.

Over the centuries Hagley Hall has entertained many important visitors – great poets, the country's top architects, scientists and politicians, including Prime Minister William Gladstone. The hall is set in some 350 acres (142ha) of imaginatively landscaped deer park, with an Ionic temple, a weathered rotunda and a folly in the form of a Gothic ruin. The Obelisk was built in 1758. Behind, the Clent Hills rise to 997ft (304m), forming the perfect backdrop for the views that will follow you along this walk.

## Aristocratic Conference Venue

Today Hagley is home to Lord and Lady Cobham and is now well established as a premier location for conferences, business meetings, product launches, fairy-tale weddings and dinner parties. It can also be visited on a guided tour.

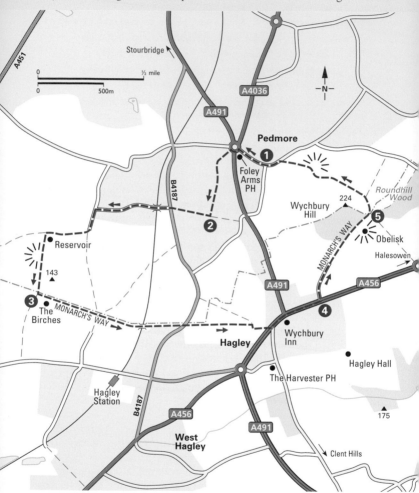

## WALK 2 DIRECTIONS

❶ From Pedmore Lane walk into the centre of Pedmore to a roundabout junction with the A491. Go around the island, cross the A491 and continue down the public bridleway signed 'Hagley

Road Nos. 280, 280A, 280B, 280C and 280D'. Follow this path along the back of houses and past a primary school then more houses, bearing right at a path junction.

❷ At the footpath T-junction, go right and continue on footpaths to the B4187 (Worcester Lane). Cross the lane and the main line railway bridge into Quarry Park Road. Continue along the path, following the public bridleway sign to Ounty John Lane, eventually turning left on to a stone track until you come to open countryside. When you reach the track junction, go right soon passing a Severn Trent reservoir. At the end of the reservoir, go immediately left and walk along a farm track over undulating ground, with views to the right towards the hills and Bewdley.

## WHILE YOU'RE THERE

Give way to the temptation of the Clent Hills and visit the country park (NT), which covers some 425 acres (172ha), to the south of this walk. Much of the area is covered with deciduous woodland, gorse and heather. Stroll up to Adam's Hill and the Four Stones where you will be rewarded with a magnificent view that, on a clear day, embraces the Shropshire, Abberley, Malvern and Welsh hills.

## WHAT TO LOOK OUT FOR

Back in the 18th century, Hagley Hall was praised for its fine gardens. Then, in the 19th century, the Kidderminster to Birmingham road (the present-day A456) was built, cutting off Wychbury Hill from the main garden, leaving the garden ornaments of the Obelisk and the Temple of Theseus on the wrong side of the road.

❸ At the junction of paths by The Birches copse, go left (east) over a stile along the North Worcestershire Path, Monarch's Way. Initially this is to the left of The Birches, then it veers to the other side of a field hedge via, a stile, descending to cross the railway line once again. It then continues through a small housing estate in Hagley, first along the estate road and then a footpath beyond No 60. Eventually the Way comes to a road corner on the

## WHERE TO EAT AND DRINK

There are three pubs along the walk route. The Foley Arms, named after the local Foley family, is in Pedmore. The Wychbury Inn in Hagley does food and is open all day. There is also the Harvester in Hagley.

B4187 (Worcester Lane). Cross the road, following the footpath sign opposite, and take the hedged path via a stile and continue ahead at the bottom of a series of fields, crossing two stiles, until you reach the busy A456. Go left alongside the road, walking to the left of the traffic island and cross the A491 (Stourbridge Road).

❹ After following the pavement along the A456 for about 350yds (320m), go left up Monument Lane. Take the lane to the end, then continue on the Monarch's Way via two gates as it climbs towards the Obelisk on Wychbury Hill. Beyond a stile the path goes to the left of the monument and along the side of Roundhill Wood to a junction of footpaths by the trees.

❺ Take the path on the left through a kissing gate and a belt of trees and, through a handgate, continue down a fenced path back to Pedmore Lane.

# Dallying in Dudley, the Capital of the Black Country

*A walk around a nature reserve near the Black Country Living Museum and Dudley Zoo.*

---

**DISTANCE** *3.5 miles (5.7km)* **MINIMUM TIME** *2hrs*

**ASCENT/GRADIENT** *82ft (25m)* ▲▲▲ **LEVEL OF DIFFICULTY** +++

**PATHS** *Parkland paths and road pavements, 3 stiles*

**LANDSCAPE** *Nature reserve and streets around Dudley*

**SUGGESTED MAP** *OS Explorer 219 Wolverhampton & Dudley*

**START/FINISH** *Grid reference: SP 949907*

**DOG FRIENDLINESS** *Off lead in park, otherwise under control*

**PARKING** *Dudley Zoo pay and display car park, Castle Hill, Dudley*

**PUBLIC TOILETS** *In Dudley*

---

The Black Country originally took its name from the dark, coal-stained soil which characterises this corner of the county where the old boundaries of Worcestershire, Shropshire, Staffordshire, and Warwickshire meet. But for many it truly earned the name in the 18th and 19th centuries, when the Industrial Revolution took off. The mines, factories and furnaces belched out their blackening soot, so the sky was 'black by day and red by night'. This walk offers the opportunity to explore the unique history of Dudley and the surrounding countryside, including Wren's Nest National Nature Reserve.

## Industrial Dudley

You could be forgiven for expecting the capital of the Black Country to be an old industrial town with little to offer the visitor, but Dudley is a large vibrant place with a fascinating history that reveals an amazing contrast of English heritage. From Saxon times up to the Civil War the town developed much like any other in Britain. In the Middle Ages it became a country market town with a town hall and small shops dotted around its central market place. The arrival of coal-mining and iron-working in the 17th century brought massive changes to the area and Dudley steadily expanded to become the main business centre of the Black Country.

It was here in the 1620s that Dud Dudley first experimented with using coal (as coke) for smelting iron. Another Dudley man, Abraham Darby, at Coalbrookdale, developed the process and the town's later ironworks dominated the area until the middle of the 20th century. The Black Country Living Museum reveals how tough life would have been during the early days of the Industrial Revolution. In the late 18th century the Stourbridge and Dudley Canal was built to link with the Staffordshire and Worcestershire Canal to the west and the rest of the Birmingham canal system.

Dudley No 1 Canal joins the Stourbridge Canal at the bottom of the Delphi Locks. Today mining activities are a thing of the past and Dudley is a clean place to live and visit. The 1817 Regency Gothic Church of St Thomas the Apostle, with its towering spire, dominates the town's skyline.

# DUDLEY

A number of other attractive old buildings remain, including the landmark Crown Inn, with its unusual bartizan (corner turret with windows), and Baylies's Charity, a charity school built in 1820 which features two enchanting statues of schoolboys dressed in the uniform of the day.

The Wren's Nest National Nature Reserve, Britain's first National Nature Reserve for Geology, is famous for its fossils, the best-known being a trilobite christened the 'Dudley Bug' or the 'Dudley Locust'. It forms the centrepiece of the town's coat of arms and is a symbol of the limestone mining industry.

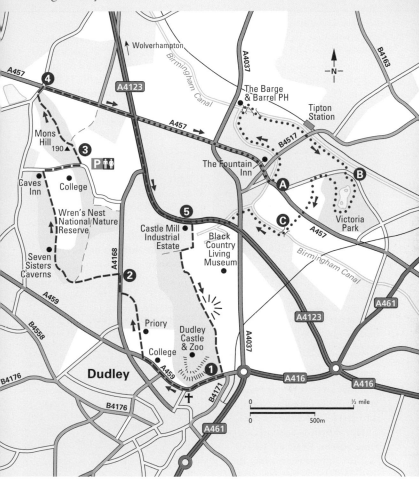

## WALK 3 DIRECTIONS

**1** From the zoo car park, stroll past the pedestrian entrance to Dudley Zoo, then at the road island bear right up The Broadway. Pass the college building and you will soon reach the 12th-century priory ruins in Priory Park. Go right and wander through to the far end of the park, then go left down Woodland Avenue, bearing right and crossing over the A4168 (Priory Road).

**2** Turn left down Cedar Road, continue past green space with swings to enter the southern

WALK

3

part of Wren's Nest National Nature Reserve over a stile, by an information board. Continue ahead for 100yds (91m), turn left up the flight of 99 steps and continue along the higher footpath, first left and then right. This path leads near to the Seven Sisters Caverns. Continue ahead and you will eventually emerge between The Caves public house and the college grounds. You are now on Wrens Hill Road near the inn. Go right along the road and just past the college buildings to a stile on the left.

## WHAT TO LOOK OUT FOR

Keep your eye open for fossils when you visit Wren's Nest National Nature Reserve. Around 425 million years ago this area was submerged, forming part of the Silurian Sea and a wide range of sea creatures, including trilobites and brachiopods, inhabited the coral reefs. Today the site has been stripped largely of its fossils – collecting is discouraged and hammers are definitely not allowed. However, there are the lime kilns to see, and children always enjoy exploring the Seven Sisters Caverns and Cherry Hole.

**3** Over the stile follow the path that takes you over craggy Mons Hill. Eventually, where the path divides, take the left fork, initially down steps, until you near some houses. Reaching Parkes Hall Road, turn right along the road until you come to the A457 (Sedgley Road West).

**4** Turn right and follow the A457 for about 750yds (686m), then go right along the A4123 (Birmingham New Road). After 0.25 mile (400m) of easy walking, the road arcs left, and beyond a bus stop look out for the Castle Mill industrial estate on the right.

**5** A few paces up the Castle Hill industrial estate access, go left through a scruffy barrier on to a footpath, then continue along the Limekiln Walk path through the woodland by Castle Hill. There are many paths through this woodland, but try to keep to the left-hand paths going southwards near to the edge of the trees for over 0.5 mile (800m). This is pleasant walking and soon the path reaches the open where it becomes a track and passes to the left of the Dudley Zoo enclosures, with a view over the Black Country Living Museum. Continue through to the zoo car park.

## WHERE TO EAT AND DRINK

A local favourite is the Caves Inn where children and dogs are allowed in the games room. Light refreshments are offered at the Black Country Living Museum and Dudley Castle. On the longer route, Walk 4, The Barge and Barrel at Tipton is a delightful canalside pub where you can enjoy the narrowboat world, or perhaps you might like a drink at The Fountain Inn at Lower Gornall, famous for its real ales, or the Waggon and Horses, Tipton.

## WHILE YOU'RE THERE

Kids will enjoy the Black Country Living Museum, which lies in the shadow of Dudley Castle. The museum is a reconstructed canalside village with a pub, shops, chapel, ironworks, miner's experience and boat trips from the wharf into the Dudley Tunnel, with its caverns and basins. Dudley Zoo, in the grounds of Dudley Castle, is a magnet for children of all ages. There are seals in the moat, llamas roaming the slopes below the keep, a tropical rain forest and Adventure Land, as well as great views to enjoy.

# Along the Birmingham Canal

*A longer walk passing close to the Black Country Living Museum.*
**See map and information panel for Walk 3**

---

**DISTANCE** *7 miles (11.3km)*  **MINIMUM TIME** *2hrs 45min*

**ASCENT/GRADIENT** *98ft (30m)* ▲▲▲  **LEVEL OF DIFFICULTY** ✦✦✦

---

## WALK 4 DIRECTIONS
## (Walk 3 option)

Follow Walk 3 as far as the A4123 (between Points ❹ and ❺), cross it and the A4037, then continue along the A457, which becomes Sedgley Road West. Just after crossing the B4517 (Owen Street), cross the canal and turn left to go down to the tow path of the Birmingham Canal and soon pass close to The Fountain pub (Point Ⓐ).

Continue along the right bank of the canal. When you get close to The Barge and Barrel pub, cross the footbridge to the left bank and go right to pass by Factory Locks. The tow path then crosses back to the right bank, via the Wood Street Footbridge. After passing by Tipton Railway Station the route goes beneath the B4517 road bridge. Leave the canal at the next road bridge, opposite a railway signal box, and go right into Watery Lane. Cross over Queen's Road into Victoria Park (Point Ⓑ), taking time to visit the park and circle the lakes where Canada geese, swans, ducks, moorhens and coots will entertain you. Exit the park and go back to Queen's Road where you turn left, then left again into Manor Road. Cross the A457, Park Lane West, into Baker Street and, at its end, cross the footbridge to descend back on to the tow path of the Birmingham Canal (Point Ⓒ).

The Birmingham Canal once carried the products of industrial Britain around the Midlands and across the country. It is part of a network of canals that makes you realise just how inventive our predecessors were. Today the canal is a leisure facility and you will see narrowboats negotiating their way up the canal in the summer.

Go right along the tow path through a gate, then bear left to go beneath the A4037, the Dudley Road Bridge, and A4123, the Birmingham New Road Bridge, which bring you near the tunnel at the rear 'Narrowboat' entrance – a direct canal link to the Black Country Living Museum. Take the opportunity to visit this fascinating outdoor attraction. Built to preserve the industrial heritage of the area, it offers an intriguing view of the Black Country as it was. Historic buildings from around the area have been rebuilt to re-create the Heart of Industrial Britain. A trip down the coal mine is a real educational experience.

Climb steps up to the A4123 and go left until you come to Castle Mill industrial estate, a road to the left. Here rejoin Walk 3 at Point ❺.

# A Walk in Leasowes Park

*From a country park into open countryside surrounding Halesowen Abbey and along a feeder canal.*

WALK

5

---

**DISTANCE** 4 miles (6.4km)   **MINIMUM TIME** 1hr 30min

**ASCENT/GRADIENT** 394ft (120m) ▲▲▲   **LEVEL OF DIFFICULTY** +++

**PATHS** Road pavements, field paths and tow path, 15 stiles

**LANDSCAPE** Nature reserve and open countryside around urban area

**SUGGESTED MAP** OS Explorer 219 Wolverhampton & Dudley

**START/FINISH** Grid reference: SP 975839

**DOG FRIENDLINESS** Off lead along tow path, otherwise under control

**PARKING** Leasowes Park car park

**PUBLIC TOILETS** None en route

---

## WALK 5 DIRECTIONS

Leave the car park at the Leasowes Park Centre at the north end by walking east past the Warden's Base building via the gate, uphill along a tarmac driveway. At the junction, near a couple of houses, bear right through a gateway and continue along the driveway past a small pool, then between the greens below Halesowen Golf Club clubhouse. Where the tarmac track arcs to the left near the clubhouse and through a gate, turn right and, at the top of the hill, the drive leads into Leasowes Lane and a residential area.

At the end of the lane, go right along Manor Lane (B4043). After passing Stennels Avenue, the lane bends sharp right. Here go left up a narrow public footpath to the right of No 61. Follow this fenced footpath into Hiplands Road; go right, then right again into Manor Abbey Road at the T-junction. In about 20yds (18m), go left down Longlands Road and continue as it bends right. After passing Lavina and Christopher roads, go left

through a public footpath barrier to reach the A456 Halesowen bypass.

Go over the busy A456 at the pedestrian crossing, taking care, and proceed down Lapal Lane opposite. After about 275yds (251m), go right over a field stile and into open countryside. Follow the direction of the fingerpost signed to Illey and take the path up along the left edge of a large field. At the top of the field, by the hedge, pause to enjoy the view to the right that embraces the Wychbury, Clent and Clee hills. Now go left over a second stile and bear right to the hedged path heading southwards. Where another path (Lye Close) joins

---

### WHERE TO EAT AND DRINK

A local favourite with walkers is The Black Horse pub in Illey. Try the excellent lasagne or perhaps a steak – the steak sauces are a speciality of the pub. It also offers a great Sunday roast. Alternatively, there is usually a mobile fast-food vehicle at the Leasowes Park Centre where you can get snacks.

from the left, the path becomes a track and the views continue through gaps to your right. At a junction of paths, continue ahead, then walk through trees to the left of Cooper's Wood. At the end of the wood, over a stile, go right, then over another stile, then bear a quarter left to a stile to cross pasture. Over a stile the path arcs right and then left over another stile on to a track.

## WHAT TO LOOK OUT FOR

Beneath the road, close to where the route leaves Lapal Lane South, is the site of Lapal Tunnel which is over 2 miles (3.2km) in length. Because it had no tow path, boats had to be 'legged' through the tunnel, which could take as long as four hours. The bargees would lie on their backs on the top of their boats, and push the barge forward by walking their feet along the tunnel roof.

Follow this track and in about 100yds (91m), go right over a pair of stiles (if you walk to the end of the track you reach a road and will find The Black Horse pub on the corner opposite). Continue to the right of a field hedge with Bartley Green football pitch on the other side. At the field corner, go left over a stile and walk around the bottom end of the football field, leaving via the football club gate on to the farm drive near Illey Hall Farm. Go left along the farm drive for 30yds (27m), then right over a stile and take the path to the left of the field hedge. Follow this path, soon merging with the Monarch's Way, over several fields and stiles, later crossing to the other side of the hedge via a stile where there is a stream to the right. The path arcs right to a bridge and becomes a farm track arcing left towards Manor Abbey Farm. Bear right and walk away from the farm,

going over a field corner stile and continuing across a large cultivated field.

Cross the stile and go left, then bear right over a footbridge to a pair of stiles that take you back to the side of the A456. As you walk, pause to enjoy a fine retrospective view of the remains of St Mary's Abbey, near Manor Abbey Farm.

Go right for 25yds (23m), then over the road at the crossing. Go right again, then left to follow the tarmac footpath at a sign, 'Leasowes Park and Breaches Pool'. This path passes along the back of residential properties. Continue ahead to right-hand of chain link fence and soon the path becomes the tow path of the Lapal Canal (formally known as the Dudley No 2). The canal is covered with water plants and there are houses up to the right. After about 400yds (366m), a bank crosses the canal, just before a former lock. Go over this bank and head along the tow path, now to the right of the canal (there is visible water here), with Leasowes Park to your right. In 150yds (137m) stop to enjoy the fine view over Breaches Pool, then continue up the tow path and return to Leasowes car park.

## WHILE YOU'RE THERE

Visit the remains of St Mary's Abbey. The abbey was founded in 1215 by monks of the Premonstratensian Order, who were granted the Manor of Hales by King John. In 1538, the abbey surrendered to the Crown. It was demolished and granted to Sir John Dudley by Henry VIII. Nearby, earth mounds and breached dams mark the place where it is believed there was once a flight of five fish ponds built by the monks to breed fish and supplement their diet.

# Woodgate Valley Country Park

*A short, easy excursion showing the West Midlands'
urban countryside at its best.*

---

**DISTANCE** 3.5 miles (5.7km)    **MINIMUM TIME** 1hr 30min

**ASCENT/GRADIENT** 49ft (15m) ▲▲▲    **LEVEL OF DIFFICULTY** ✦✦✦

**PATHS** Grassy footpaths and tracks, no stiles

**LANDSCAPE** Country park

**SUGGESTED MAP** OS Explorers 219 Wolverhampton & Dudley; 220 Birmingham

**START/FINISH** Grid reference: SP 995829 (on Explorer 219)

**DOG FRIENDLINESS** Off lead around park

**PARKING** Woodgate Valley Country Park

**PUBLIC TOILETS** Country Park visitor centre building

---

Birmingham is surrounded by country parks, which act as the lungs of the city. Woodgate Valley Country Park is one of these vital green spaces and this walk takes you past an urban farm complex and along the side of the babbling Bourn Brook, which runs the length of the valley to the River Rea at Cannon Hill Park.

## Woodgate Valley Country Park

The park comprises some 450 acres (182ha) of meadows, hedgerows and woodland on the western edge of Birmingham. It was originally a mixture of farms and smallholdings and every effort has been made to retain its rural appeal. Threatened by development, it was designated a Country Park in 1984. A programme of hedge and tree replanting has taken place and the visitor centre opened in 1987.

The woodland, ponds and meadows have now become home to a vast range of wildlife and hundreds of species of plants and flowers. The meadowlands near the start of this walk, known as Pinewoods, are a treat to stroll through on a warm summer's day. Pheasants, kingfishers, cuckoos, chiffchaffs, whitethroats and willow warblers are regular visitors, and, if you're lucky, you may see a long-eared owl or even a marsh harrier. When the plants are in flower, butterflies arrive in large numbers and some 20 species have been seen during a normal summer. Look out especially for the red admiral and the small tortoiseshell.

During 2001, the foot and mouth epidemic resulted in the closure of many footpaths in the Midlands countryside and Woodgate Valley Park became a refuge for walkers and ramblers from outlying areas. Although it is close to so many urban roads, you can still enjoy peace and tranquillity away from the noise of traffic. Houses surround it, yet very few can be seen when you are walking the footpaths along the side of Bourn Brook.

## Underground Canal

Beneath the parkland are the remains of part of the Lapal Tunnel (see Walk 5) on the Dudley No 2 Canal, which connected Halesowen with Selly

# WOODGATE

Oak. It is one of the longest canal tunnels in England and a reminder that the industrial side of Birmingham is never too far away, even if you can't actually see it. The canal was built in 1790 despite fierce local opposition as industrial expansion in the West Midlands was proceeding at a frightening pace. Measuring only 9ft (2.7m) wide and 9ft (2.7m) from water level to ceiling, it gradually fell into disuse with competition from the railways. Following mining subsidence in 1917, the tunnel was closed and finally sealed off in 1926, though there is an active campaign to reopen it sometime in the future.

WALK 6

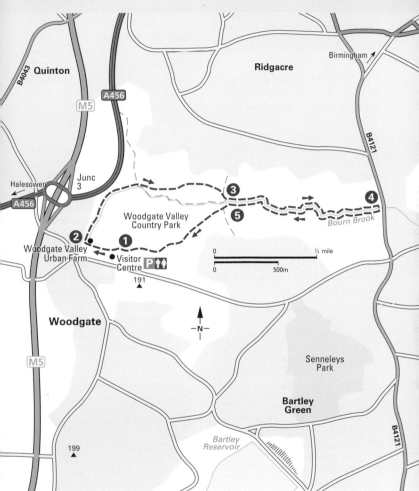

## WALK 6 DIRECTIONS

❶ Walk from the car park at the visitor centre down to the Woodgate Valley Urban Farm. Go left via the gate between the animal enclosures and then descend to a kissing gate.

❷ When you reach the farm access lane, cross it and go right, along the tarmac footpath by the side of a stream – the Bourn Brook – with the bridlepath up to the left. This path arcs right, around the edge of the park until you reach a second footbridge

WALK

6

## WHERE TO EAT AND DRINK

Woodgate Valley Café, in the visitor centre, is a popular eating place for walkers, offering sandwiches, toasties, jacket potatoes, curries and Cornish pasties. There are picnic tables and benches in the park area where children and dogs are always welcome. The Old Crown is in Carter's Lane if you would prefer a pint, but children and dogs are not admitted.

over the brook. At this footbridge, do not cross it but bear left past the large oak tree and a bench seat and walk along a footpath that arcs away from the stream towards an area of young trees. This is easy, pleasant walking and in about 150yds (137m) you will come to a junction of footpaths. Continue left ahead (if you go right you will return to the Bourn Brook), keeping to the right of the young trees as you progress in a generally easterly direction on the grass path that meanders along the edge of the trees.

## WHILE YOU'RE THERE

The Lickey Hills Country Park is just 7 miles (11.3km) down the M5 motorway. Although it's in Worcestershire, this is another playground popular with people from Birmingham. From Beacon Hill there is one of the most spectacular views across the whole of the West Midlands. At the visitor centre in Warren Lane you can enjoy a fine sculpture trail, a large play area for the children and superb woodland.

❸ Another footpath comes in from the left and you then reach another junction of footpaths at which you continue ahead. Soon another path merges from the left and you bear right towards a rather high footbridge over the stream. Do not cross it, instead bear left and follow the footpath on the left side of Bourn Brook. This leads into the trees and there follows a very pleasant stroll through the park, always close to the bank of the stream (ignore a second footbridge).

❹ All too soon you will hear the noise of traffic on the B4121 ahead. Just before you reach the road, go right over the footbridge and follow the footpath down the other side of the stream. The path passes close to housing, but this is barely visible and the country feel is maintained until you reach the high footbridge once again.

❺ Do not go over the footbridge but leave the Bourn Brook behind and bear half left to take a grassy footpath that crosses open land diagonally with houses to your left (do not go left towards the houses). Through a tree belt maintain your direction over a second open area, diverging away from the houses. At the end, cross the footbridge in the far corner and bear right to follow the path near the field edge, firstly in woods, then passing by a football pitch to arrive back at the visitor centre.

## WHAT TO LOOK OUT FOR

Look out for some rare and unusual breeds of farm animals at the Woodgate Valley Urban Farm, as well as domestic animals, birds and pets. The farm is a registered charity, maintained by volunteers from the local community. If pony trekking is your scene, Hole Farm Pony Trekking Centre offers facilities for riders of all ages and abilities.

# Mines and Monasteries in Sandwell Valley Park

*An easy walk around an RSPB nature reserve and a fine country park reveals a legacy of agriculture and industry.*

| | |
|---|---|
| **DISTANCE** 4.5 miles (7.2km) | **MINIMUM TIME** 2hrs |
| **ASCENT/GRADIENT** 66ft (20m) ▲▲▲ | **LEVEL OF DIFFICULTY** +++ |
| **PATHS** Lakeside paths and tracks, no stiles | |
| **LANDSCAPE** Country park with many lakes | |
| **SUGGESTED MAP** OS Explorer 220 Birmingham | |
| **START/FINISH** Grid reference: SP 035927 | |
| **DOG FRIENDLINESS** Off lead in park | |
| **PARKING** RSPB visitor centre | |
| **PUBLIC TOILETS** None en route | |

Once upon a time there was a 12th-century Benedictine monastery on the site of an earlier hermitage in the area now called Sandwell Valley Country Park, situated at the north-seastern edge of West Bromwich. The monastery was closed down in 1525 on the directions of Cardinal Wolsey, then in 1705 Sandwell Hall was erected on the site for the Earl of Dartmouth, incorporating some of the old priory buildings. The hall was demolished in 1928 with the development of Hamstead Colliery, which came to dominate the whole area. When the pit was nationalised in the 1940s it was one of the largest in South Staffordshire, outside Cannock Chase, with nearly 1,000 men working underground here and at the nearby Sandwell Park Colliery.

## From Colliery to Country Park

The collieries closed in the early 1960s, since when the land has been transformed into an urban oasis. The earthworks and spoil from the site became a series of artificial lakes and landscaped to produce an amazingly different scene. Sandwell Valley Country Park is now a fascinating area of lakes and 2,000 acres (810ha) of parkland developed from the old colliery sites and the remains of the Sandwell Hall Estate. The park has become a major leisure facility, with three golf courses, walking routes, a Millennium Cycle Route and two off-road cycle paths, which have been specially designed for mountain bikes. Around 20,000 people visit the park each year. Wildfowl flock to the area in large numbers and the Royal Society for the Protection of Birds (RSPB) has established a nature reserve near by, which covers some 25 acres (10ha) of the reclaimed Hamstead Colliery site (see What to Look Out For).

## Victorian Farm

Forge Mill visitor centre can be found on the other side of Forge Lane, and Swan Pool leads to footbridges over the noisy M5 motorway. Sandwell Park Farm was also part of the Earl of Dartmouth's estate and was extensively restored in 1981 to show the traditional Victorian methods of farming. The farm has a walled kitchen garden, craft shops, a rare breeds area and a heritage centre where you can see the findings of a 1980s archaeological dig at Sandwell Priory. There are also toilets and tea rooms (see Where to Eat and Drink).

## WALK 7 DIRECTIONS

❶ Leave the RSPB car park by going left of the visitor centre building on to a footpath. This leads down to a path along the dike crest between the River Tame and Forge Mill Lake. Continue along this footpath which arcs gently right and look out for the many birds on the lake, as well as Canada geese and ducks on the river. As you work your way around the lake you will come to a gateway where you go left over a

bridge across the River Tame and turn immediately left to continue on a tarmac path/cycleway that leads down to Forge Lane.

❷ Cross the busy lane with great care, and walk to the right of the Sandwell Sailing Club premises, then bear left until you come to the shore of Swan Pool.

❸ Here turn left and stroll around the side of the pool for 150yds (137m), then bear left again on a footpath, via a kissing

### WHILE YOU'RE THERE

Take the opportunity to travel into West Bromwich. It is the centre of the new Metropolitan Borough of Sandwell and is a clean, attractive town, with a fine modern centre, far removed from the smoky and dirty 'boom' town it was in the 19th century. Situated in the old historic part of town is the superb timber-framed Old Manor House, which is now a restaurant.

gate, that leads across meadowland away from the water's edge, initially alongside the Pool's fence. Through a kissing gate, cross the track and continue ahead on a hedged footpath heading generally south-west. At a junction of paths go left through a barrier and proceed through the trees, then go right to follow the path to the north bank of both Cypress and Ice House pools. Continue ahead to leave the lakes and emerge on a concrete lane by the side of the noisy M5. (If you had continued ahead at the junction of paths instead of going left, you would have arrived at the same position.) Go left and stroll along this wide lane. At a junction, bear right and take the footbridge to cross over the M5.

### WHAT TO LOOK OUT FOR

The RSPB Visitor Centre in Sandwell Valley Country Park is an important West Midlands home to a wide variety of birds and attracts around 150 species of birds each year. There are leaflets, available in the visitor centre, describing the birds you might see in the park. Can you spot a tufted duck, a little ringed plover, a whitethroat, a snipe, a reed warbler or perhaps a wader? Also look out for sheep-shearing demonstrations and rare and common livestock at Sandwell Park Farm.

❹ Across the bridge go right down steps, now on the Beacon Way, and wind amid trees on the path up to Sandwell Park Farm where there are toilet facilities and you can get light refreshments.

❺ Leave the farm through the car park and continue along the lane, turning right opposite a building through a kissing gate and walk ahead along the signed public footpath heading north-eastwards within a belt of trees. (To the left you will see a golf practice area.) When you reach the end of the hedged area, bear left and proceed along a tarmac path, signed 'Swan Pool and Forge Mill Farm', until you reach a junction.

### WHERE TO EAT AND DRINK

Children are welcomed in the tea rooms of Sandwell Park Farm, but not dogs. A Sandwell Valley full English breakfast will sustain even the hungriest walker and is available until 2:30pm every day, or perhaps you would prefer a jacket potato, pasty, pie or a salad. To quench your thirst you could visit one of the many pubs in West Bromwich, 3 miles (4.8km) west.

❻ Go right here along Salters Lane and return over the M5, via a second footbridge. Take the tarmac path that goes to the left of Swan Pool and continue left past the sailing cub premises to busy Forge Lane. Cross the lane and take the footpath back to the bridge over the River Tame to reach the junction of footpaths by the edge of Forge Mill Lake.

❼ Go left and walk around the lake, leaving the River Tame and going right just before the railway bridge. Keep close to the lake shore until turning left at a sign, this path takes you back to the visitor centre.

# Hay Head Wood and the Walsall Waterfront

*Along the Wyrley and Essington, and Rushall canals
to Park Lime Pits Local Nature Reserve.*

---

**DISTANCE** 3.75 *miles (6km)*   **MINIMUM TIME** *1hr 15min*

**ASCENT/GRADIENT** *66ft (20m)* ▲▲▲   **LEVEL OF DIFFICULTY** +++

**PATHS** *Field paths and tow paths, no stiles*

**LANDSCAPE** *Canalside and urban parkland*

**SUGGESTED MAP** *OS Explorer 220 Birmingham*

**START/FINISH** *Grid reference: SK 041910*

**DOG FRIENDLINESS** *Off lead along tow path, otherwise under control*

**PARKING** *Hay Head Wood Nature Reserve car park*

**PUBLIC TOILETS** *None en route*

---

As you explore the history of the Black Country, it becomes clear that Walsall was very much at the hub of the Industrial Revolution in 19th-century Britain. Each large town in the area had its role to play, and limestone, used as flux in the iron foundries and for cement production in the construction of canal buildings, was mined in the countryside around Walsall. The town also became England's centre for the manufacture of leather goods and fine saddlery – the nickname of the local football team is the Saddlers. Much of old Walsall has disappeared, but it has become a vibrant modern town, surrounded by numerous parks, which offer a link with its industrial past.

### The 'Curly Wyrley' and the Rushall

John Wilkinson, a famous pioneering 'ironmaster' opened up Hay Head Wood for limestone excavation in the 18th century. It was transported along two canals – the Wyrley and Essington, and the Rushall. The Wyrley and Essington was completed in 1797, with nine locks designed to lift the lime-laden barges some 65ft (20m) up to the Longwood Junction near Aldridge. This contour canal, affectionately known as 'The Curly Wyrley', follows the lie of the land and winds its way from Hay Head Park up to Lime Pits Farm and Park Lime Pits Local Nature Reserve, then on to the north of Birmingham. The Rushall Canal was built as a 2.5-mile (4km) connection between the Wyrley and Essington Canal and the Tame Valley Canal.

Limestone extraction finally ceased in the 1920s, but remnants of the canal wharf buildings, pit shafts and pump housings can still be seen. The land around the lime pits have since been reclaimed by nature.

### In the Footsteps of Heavy Horses

The walk starts from the Hay Head Wood Nature Reserve and proceeds along the tow path of the Rushall Canal where once horses pulled heavily laden narrowboats of limestone to flux mills and cement factories in the Black Country. It continues through the recreation ground near to Walsall's

# WALSALL

famous arboretum, passes through an urban area, then crosses farm fields to Riddian Bridge before finishing along the great and pleasant tow path of the Wyrley and Essington Canal.

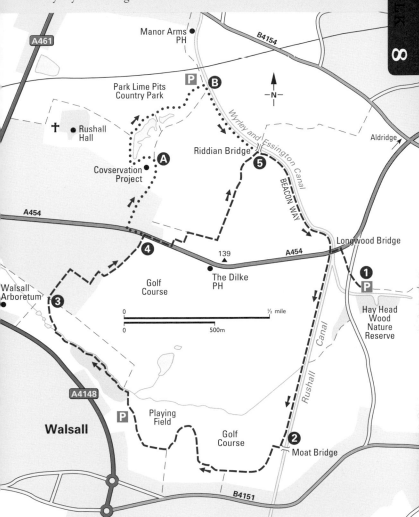

## WALK 8 DIRECTIONS

**1** From the car park proceed over Longwood Lane, now on the Beacon Way, through a parking area on to the Longwood Bridge. Cross it to descend left to the tow path of the Rushall Canal. Go right (south-west) and walk past the canal junction, now off the Beacon Way, along the side of the very straight part of the canal.

**2** After 1100yds (1000m) you will come to Moat Bridge over the canal where you go off to the right along hedged track and, at a metalled path, go left (south) along the left (or right) side of the hedge. At the end of the field, go right and join a footpath that leads around the bottom end of a golf course. Follow the blue-topped white posts and continue past the rear of gardens, with the

29

golf course to your right, and along the back of playing fields. After passing a sports pavilion and an exit area to the B4151, continue ahead over a footbridge on a metalled track that leads to the municipal golf course's main car park and a large recreational space. Leave the car park at its rear by the dog walk sign board, and continue along a tarmac path by the left side of a stream. After about 700yds (640m), turn right over the stone footbridge, and walk to the right-hand side of a childrens play area up to reach a tarmac driveway.

**3** Head right, up the driveway to leave the park area, then cross over Buchanan Road and continue up the footpath until you reach Argyle Road. Go right along Argyle Road which arcs left, and look out for a footpath sign. Go right and take the hedged/fenced footpath along the back of the houses in Fernleigh Road. This emerges on to the A454 (Aldridge Road/Mellish Road).

### WHILE YOU'RE THERE

The Walsall Arboretum, off the corner of Lichfield Street and Broadway North, was formed in 1874 by the Walsall Arboretum and Lake Company. They rented 7 acres (2.8ha) of land from the landowners, Lord Hatherton and Sir George Mellish, to provide a facility for croquet, archery and quoits, with two lakes for angling and boating.

**4** Cross over the A454 and go right along Aldridge Road's grass verge for some 220yds (201m), then go left over a stile by a footpath sign to Riddian Bridge. Continue along the footpath to the right of a farm building and then follow a series of fingerposts until you come to Riddian Bridge on the Wyrley and Essington Canal.

### WHERE TO EAT AND DRINK

Marston Pedigree and Banks's real ales are on offer at the traditional Manor Arms, near Park Lime Pits Country Park. Children and dogs are made very welcome at this popular pub where Sunday lunch is a special treat. Alternatively, you could try The Dilke pub along the A454 (Aldridge Road) or one of the many pubs, restaurants and eateries in Walsall itself.

**5** Descend to the tow path, which is part of the Beacon Way, turn right and walk along it. This is easy walking, with just a few ducks and perhaps a heron or two for company. You may see fishermen on the banks of the canal attempting to catch some of the roach, tench, carp and pike that live in the waters. In about 0.5 mile (800m) you come to Longwood Bridge. Beyond the bridge, exit on to Beacon Way and the A454. Cross the canal and bear right to return to the car park at the nature reserve.

### WHAT TO LOOK OUT FOR

The area around Park Lime Pits Local Nature Reserve has become a haven for wildlife. Over 100 bird species have been recorded here. Moorhens, coots, mallards and grebes can be seen around the clear pools near the reed beds, while bullfinches and buntings inhabit the stubble fields, which are specially managed to encourage wildlife. Although industrial in origin, the site has actually changed very little since the last pits were worked more than 170 years ago. The water quality in the deep pools is so good that freshwater crayfish, endangered elsewhere in the country, flourish here.

# The Walsall Countryside

*A longer walk taking in more lime pits and an environmental farm.*
**See map and information panel for Walk 8**

| DISTANCE 4.75 miles (7.7km) | MINIMUM TIME 1hr 45min |
|---|---|
| ASCENT/GRADIENT 66ft (20m) ▲▲▲ | LEVEL OF DIFFICULTY +++ |

## WALK 9 DIRECTIONS
### (Walk 8 option)

After crossing the A454 at Point **4**, go left along the pavement of Mellish Road up to Mellish Drive. Turn right and walk to the end of Mellish Drive and a kissing gate. Continue into open countryside on the footpath. You will pass between designated stubble fields where the stubble is left after the harvest to provide a suitable environment for local birdlife – yellow hammers, reed buntings and a variety of finches feed on the leftover grain. The farmer is pioneering a conservation project leaving strips of land free from pesticides and fertilisers in order to encourage wildlife back to his 57 acres (23ha) of grass, wheat and barley fields. As you walk along, notice the abundance of wild flowers are growing around the field edges.

When you reach a waymarked junction of footpaths, bear left through the fence gap into the trees of Park Lime Pits Local Nature Reserve (Point **A**). Follow the footpath to the main pool where you go left up steps to follow the path along the pool edge. You may pass people fishing for the large carp and pike that frequent the pool. From 1417 to the mid-19th century limestone was burnt here to make lime, and this was dispatched across Britain via the Rushall Canal and the wider canal system. Following the demise of the lime industry, the pits were closed in 1865 and planted with trees. Today they have been flooded to make an attractive leisure place for local people.

At the far end of the pool descend steps and bear left up further steps to progress into the open, looking south-west to see Rushall Hall and St Michael's Church. The hall was mentioned as the Manor in the Domesday Book but was dismantled after the Civil War. It was rebuilt in 1846. James Cranston built St Michael's Church in 1856 and its fine spire was added in 1867. Take the left fork and continue north eastwards alongside a well laid hedge until you reach Lime Pits car park via a kissing gate by the side of the Wyrley and Essington Canal (Point **B**), via another kissing gate.

At the canal, go right and walk along the tow path of the contour canal. This is easy walking with pleasant views all around. You may see the cattle in the fields opposite drinking from the canal. At Riddian Bridge, rejoin the route of Walk 8 at Point **5**.

WALK 10

# The Jewellery Quarter

*Follow the canal system into one of Birmingham's most famous areas.*

| | |
|---|---|
| **DISTANCE** 4 miles (6.4km) | **MINIMUM TIME** 1hr 45min |
| **ASCENT/GRADIENT** 16ft (5m) ▲▲▲ | **LEVEL OF DIFFICULTY** ✦✦✦ |

**PATHS** Tow paths and street pavements, no stiles

**LANDSCAPE** Canals, historic buildings and manufacturing area

**SUGGESTED MAP** OS Explorer 220 Birmingham, or AA Street by Street: Birmingham, Wolverhampton

**START/FINISH** Grid reference: SP 065686

**DOG FRIENDLINESS** On lead at all times

**PARKING** Northwood Street pay-and-display car park

**PUBLIC TOILETS** Vyse Street

## WALK 10 DIRECTIONS

In the 16th century, Birmingham was merely a market town in the heart of the English countryside, surrounded by forests and common land. The Industrial Revolution changed this for ever and, following huge expansion, Queen Victoria granted Birmingham a city charter in 1889. Expansion continued as it grew into the second largest city in Britain.

During this period the city also acquired an amazing network of canals (more than Venice) which became the transport hub for the whole of England, allowing the transportation of manufactured goods far and wide. One of the 1,200 trades that flourished in the city was jewellery manufacturing. Precious metals had been worked here since the 14th century, and the 18th century saw the development of the now famous Jewellery Quarter, and by the 20th century, some 30,000 people were involved in the business. The network of streets and craftworkers' shops still survives and has been designated a conservation area. This walk takes in the Jewellery Quarter, and includes a tour of some of the superb buildings that survive in the city centre.

From the car park, walk down Northwood Street and go left into Caroline Street. At the end of the street, continue ahead into the churchyard of St Paul's Church, the so-called Jeweller's Church, then walk up Ludgate Hill. Proceed over the Birmingham and Frazeley Canal and cross the footbridge over Great Charles Street Queensway. Continue up Church Street and

WHERE TO EAT AND DRINK

As you pass close to St Paul's Square, call in at The Rope Walk for a pint and a snack – look out for the chef's special. Children and guide dogs are welcome. There are numerous eating places around Brindley Place and the Gas Street Basin. If you fancy a steak try The Wharf (children and guide dogs also welcome).

# BIRMINGHAM

into Colmore Row to see the impressive Birmingham Cathedral (St Philip's). Inside there are magnificent stained-glass windows by Sir Edward Burne-Jones.

Walk along Colmore Row into Victoria Square, passing by the Museum and Art Gallery/Town Hall and Council House. Bear right into Paradise Forum past the Central Library, then cross the walkway into Centenary Square to see the Repertory Theatre, the Hall of Memory and the International Convention Centre buildings. At Symphony Hall go left, across Broad Street, into Bridge Street. Go right in 100yds (91m) to descend to the Worcester and Birmingham Canal, and the Gas Street Basin. Go left past The Brindley and cross the canal, via a mooring pontoon and a footbridge, before going right along the tow path past the Tap and Spile pub and beneath Broad Street to Water's Edge, passing the National Sea Life Centre in Brindley Place.

Continue ahead over a footbridge and beneath a footbridge numbered 68 along the tow path beneath Sheepcote Street Bridge to St Vincent Bridge. Cross it and descend to the tow path on the other side of the Birmingham Main Line Canal, heading back towards the city centre. There are usually narrowboats moored by the canal edge as you walk to the Old Turn Junction, where the Worcester

and Birmingham, the Birmingham Main Line, and the Birmingham and Frazeley canals meet.

Bear left at the junction and walk along the left-hand bank tow path of the Birmingham and Frazeley Canal, passing the National Indoor Arena building and beneath Tindal Bridge – ahead is the British Telecom Tower. Descend past a flight of eight canal locks and, just before the ninth lock, go left through a gap in the wall and up steps, signed 'Jewellery Quarter', into Newhall Street.

Go left along Newhall Street which becomes Graham Street, then right along Frederick Street past the Argent Centre to see the Jewellery Quarter clock tower. The Chamberlain Clock was erected in 1903 to honour one of Birmingham's favourite sons and respected public servants, Joseph Chamberlain, who did much to champion the jewellers' cause. Turn left into Warstone Lane, then just after passing the gateway to the Warstone Lane Cemetery, go right up a pathway into the cemetery past the catacombs to Pitsford Street. Go right to Vyse Street, then left to the main Jewellery Quarter. Continue right into Hockley Street and then go to the right of the Jewellers Arms pub down Spencer Street, bear right into Caroline Street, then go left to return along Northwood Street to the car park.

*Overleaf: Canal boats moored along the banks, Gas Street Basin in Birmingham (Walk 10)*

WALK
11

# A Priory Appointment at Studley

*A walk through typical Warwickshire countryside, passing a former castle and the site of a 12th-century priory.*

| | |
|---|---|
| **DISTANCE** 5 miles (8km) | **MINIMUM TIME** 2hr 15min |
| **ASCENT/GRADIENT** 49ft (15m) ▲▲▲ | **LEVEL OF DIFFICULTY** +++ |

**PATHS** Field paths and parkland, no stiles

**LANDSCAPE** Gentle rolling countryside

**SUGGESTED MAP** OS Explorer 220 Birmingham

**START/FINISH** Grid reference: SP 071637

**DOG FRIENDLINESS** Under control at all times

**PARKING** Pool Road car park, Studley

**PUBLIC TOILETS** Bottom of High Street, Studley

Although mentioned in the Domesday Book, very little of ancient Studley remains. The village is built on the old Roman Ryknild Street, which became the main turnpike into Birmingham in 1721. The River Arrow still meanders gently through pastureland below the residential areas.

The mill, an old castle, manor house and church are the only old buildings to survive. Washford Mill has become a public house. The present extraordinary neo-norman and Neo-Gothic Studley Castle were actually built in 1834, as the home of the Goodricke family and is now a prestigious hotel. Of its 13th-century predecessor nothing remains. The manor house, which is now called Mountbatten House, used to be the headquarters of the Royal Life Saving Society before it moved down the road to Broom, near Alcester. The 700-year-old Church of the Nativity of the Blessed Virgin Mary, on the other side of the river away from the village, features a Norman door, an old rood, some ancient stairs and a stone coffin lid displaying a superb cross. A fascinating brass relates the story of a commendable 17th-century local man who left money for 48 penny loaves for the poor to be distributed every Sunday.

## Studley's Trade and Industry

Needle-making became the main occupation in Studley from the early 17th century, when Elizabeth I allowed a group of Hugenot refugees from France to settle in the area. They brought with them the craft of precision making needles, which had been developed by continental manufacturers in the late medieval period. Their expertise helped the local industry develop and soon Studley was one of the largest producers of needles in Britain and known worldwide. From the mid-19th century, surgical needles were greatly in demand. By the end of the 19th century industrial techniques had taken over and there were over 3,000 workers involved in the needle-making business. Since then the industry has declined, though there is still the need for precision needles and they continue to be made in some of the local factories. It is this industry we must thank for Studley having more public houses than most villages to supply refreshment to the factory workers.

# STUDLEY

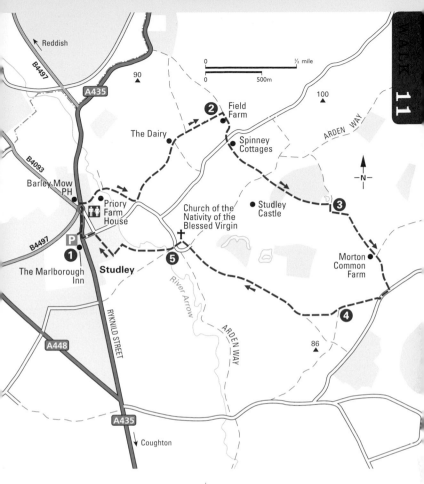

## WALK 11 DIRECTIONS

❶ From the Pool Road Car Park walk down the footpath beside the Studley Community Infants School and continue ahead down Needle Close to the Alcester road, then go left to the roundabout. Cross over the road and go down the drive to Priory Court, then via a kissing gate on a footpath to the left of houses. Cross the footbridge over the River Arrow and, through a kissing gate, bear right to another into a large field, aiming towards a second kissing gate at the corner of the field opposite. Don't go through it but head left to cross the

pasture diagonally, aiming to the left of a field gate in the hedge to a waymarker, then go right alongside the field hedge for about 0.5 mile (800m).

❷ Through a kissing gate and then a hand gate, go right between the buildings of Field Farm and walk along the farm drive. In about 100yds (91m), go right through a gate crossing the corner of the field on to Hardwick Lane via a kissing gate. Cross the lane and, through a gate, walk between Spinney Cottages, then through a kissing gate to walk ahead over parkland until you come to a driveway near some glasshouses,

*37*

reaching it via a kissing gate and two hand gates. Cross the driveway, go through a handgate and walk to the right of a cottage to enter the wood via two gates. Follow the footpath through the trees and, through another gate, then continue ahead by the field edge until you reach the end of the woodland. Turn left and walk up a farm track past a duck pond and towards a farm building.

❸ Opposite the pond, go right on a track and after 90 paces, go left across the field, aiming for an oak tree. Through the hedge gap, go half right and cross the next cultivated field diagonally to a footbridge, then, through a gate, continue alongside a wire fence to a gate, then alongside a hedge, to pass to the left of Morton Common Farm. Reaching the farm drive follow it to a road. Go right along the road for about 150yds (137m), then right again over a footbridge and go half left through a young wood. At the farm gate, bear right and walk alongside the stream until you reach a farm track.

❹ Through a field gate continue right along the track. In about 0.5 mile (800m), it arcs right; turn left here by gates and an old oak to cross the middle of the field towards Studley's Church of the Nativity of the Blessed Virgin Mary. Go through the overflow graveyard, via two hand, gates and enter the main churchyard via another, passing the church and leaving via the gate with the lamp over it on to a lane.

❺ Go briefly left and cross the lane to go through a kissing gate. Descend through pastureland, cross the footbridge over the River Arrow, then bear right and walk along the river bank towards Studley. A kissing gate leads into the end of Wickham Road. Head left along the side of the housing estate and bear right into Gunners Lane. Continue ahead and, after a path section, go left up Castle Road to the Alcester road, cross and go briefly right and then left to ascend Needle Close to the car park at the start of the walk.

# Around the Roman Town of Alcester

*An easy walk through an old Roman town,*
*picturesque woodland and attractive villages.*

---

DISTANCE *5.5 miles (8.8km)*  MINIMUM TIME *2hr 15 min*

ASCENT/GRADIENT *269ft (82m)* ▲▲▲  LEVEL OF DIFFICULTY ✦✦✦

PATHS *Pavements, field paths, woodland tracks and farm lanes, 3 stiles*

LANDSCAPE *Gentle rolling farmland, woodland and rural town*

SUGGESTED MAP *OS Explorer 205 Stratford-upon-Avon & Evesham*

START/FINISH *Grid reference: SP 088572*

DOG FRIENDLINESS *Under control at all times*

PARKING *Bleachfield Street car park, Alcester*

PUBLIC TOILETS *Bulls Head Yard car park, Alcester*

---

Alcester is one of the most delightful towns in Warwickshire. This former Roman settlement has sadly lost its ancient abbey, but the abbot's splendid ivory crozier, which was discovered in the rectory garden, is now displayed in the British Museum. From time to time new Roman relics also come to light, such as the Roman milestone commemorating the Emperor Constantine (AD 306–337), which was excavated in the town in 1966. The Romano-British town, which flourished between the 2nd and 4th centuries AD is now completely covered by the modern town.

## Major Transport Artery

Following the turnpiking of the Stratford to Alcester road in 1753, Alcester became a busy stopping point on the main stagecoach route linking London and Holyhead via Shrewsbury. Few of the town's old coaching inns survived the developments of the 1960s, but the Swan, Bear and White Lion are reminders of those days. Horse-drawn coaches gave way to trains, but today Alcester's old station is all that remains in the age of the car.

## Blooming Alcester

The town centre is now bypassed and so Alcester has had the space to spruce itself up. A national winner of the Britain in Bloom competition, the residents adorn its streets each year with beautiful flowers, making the High Street particularly attractive. The great tower of St Nicholas dominates the centre with its clock face set at an angle on the corner of its tower. The Market Hall was originally built in 1618, when it was simply a pillared edifice, but a timber-framed upper storey was added in 1641. In 1874 the arches were filled in and today it is occupied by the Town Hall.

## Forest of Arden

The walk takes you through the old part of Alcester and down Malt Mill Lane into Oversley Green. Beautiful Oversley Wood is a remnant of the original Forest of Arden and, if you walk through here in spring you will be greeted by a carpet of bluebells and may even spot a shy muntjac deer. The route goes close to the delightful villages of Exhall and Wixford, with their black-and-white buildings, then returns over Primrose Hill, which rises 350ft (107m) above the Arrow Valley, offering a fine view of Ragley Hall (see While You're There) to the left. Once over the busy A46 road you will pass several beautiful thatched cottages as you walk down Primrose Lane on the way back into Oversley Green.

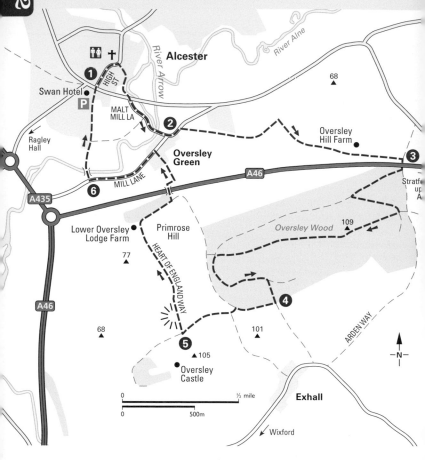

## WALK 12 DIRECTIONS

❶ From the car park enter Bleachfield Street and go left to the old Stratford Road. Cross the road and wander up High Street. Bear right past impressive St Nicholas Church and, at the corner of the road, turn right down Malt Mill Lane. At the bottom of the lane, go left through the public gardens and follow the tarmac footpath by the side of the River Arrow to

reach the old Stratford Road again. Cross the road and go down the lane opposite into Oversley Green village, crossing the bridge over the River Arrow.

❷ At the road junction bear left on Stratford Road and in 80yds (73m) go right along a hedged footpath behind a row of houses. Cross a field via two kissing gates and walk past a golf driving range, crossing a stile to reach a kissing

# ALCESTER

## WHAT TO LOOK OUT FOR

The lovely Church of St Milburga, on the edge of Wixford village, is tucked away up a high banked lane and is almost hidden from view by the oldest yew tree in Warwickshire. Look especially for the 1411 Crewe brass, which lies on top of a tomb in the south chapel. The 5ft (1.5m) long tomb shows Thomas Crewe, who looked after the affairs of the Countess of Warwick, wearing armour.

❹ Go right and walk along the edge of Oversley Wood to its corner. Continue ahead along the hedged track until you reach a farm lane, with Oversley Castle on the hillock to the left.

❺ Go right along the lane and join the Heart of England Way. Walk up the lane towards some large grain silos by the side of Lower Oversley Lodge Farm. From the farm complex go right along the concrete lane and left through a handgate down to the footbridge over the busy A46. Cross and walk down Primrose Lane, passing a beautiful thatched house. At the T-junction go left along Mill Lane for about 650yds (594m).

gate at a junction of paths. Do not go through it but go right here along the field edge, then through a field gate and across pastureland to join a track that passes through a kissing gate below Oversley Hill Farm before coming to a Severn Trent sub station.

❸ Continue ahead across a stile and through a gate to go right, under the A46 road bridge, and bear right through the gateway into Oversley Wood. Take the metalled track into the wood for about 400yds (366m), then go left. In a further 400yds (366m) the metalled track arcs right. At a path crossroads, go right on a grass path steeply uphill and continue westwards over the crest of the hill, descending past a viewpoint bench back to the main metalled track. Now go left for 650yds (594m), then right at a bench onto a wide path to leave the wood over a stile.

❻ After passing a fourth mobile home, go right, down a path and cross a footbridge over the River Arrow. Continuing ahead, the path becomes a lane by houses, with allotments to the right. Walk up Bleachfield Street back to the car park.

## WHERE TO EAT AND DRINK

Alcester has a large number of public houses and eating places. The Bleachfield Street car park is at the rear of The Swan Hotel, a regular drinking hole for walkers. You'll be made very welcome and can enjoy great home-cooked meals at reasonable prices and a good selection of beers. Children and dogs are allowed in the bar area.

## WHILE YOU'RE THERE

Take the opportunity to visit Ragley Hall, along the Evesham Road, set in 400 acres (165ha) of parkland. The home of the Marquess and Marchioness of Hertford, it was designed by Robert Hooke in 1680, and is one of the earliest and most handsome of England's great Palladian houses. The magnificent great hall contains some outstanding baroque plasterwork by James Gibbs and a large mural up the stairway. The stables house a carriage collection and 'Capability' Brown designed the delightful gardens. There is also an adventure playground for children. Open Thursday to Sunday, 11am–6pm, daily during the school holidays.

# The Shakespeare Connection

*Along the banks of the River Avon, from a village frequented by Shakespeare into the Warwickshire countryside.*

| | |
|---|---|
| **DISTANCE** 7 miles (11.3km) | **MINIMUM TIME** 3hrs |
| **ASCENT/GRADIENT** 190ft (58m) ▲▲▲ | **LEVEL OF DIFFICULTY** ✦✦✦ |

**PATHS** Field paths, farm tracks and country lanes, 1 stile

**LANDSCAPE** Riverside and rolling countryside

**SUGGESTED MAP** OS Explorer 205 Stratford-upon-Avon & Evesham

**START/FINISH** Grid reference: SP 098518

**DOG FRIENDLINESS** On lead at all times

**PARKING** Car park south-east of roundabout in Bidford-on-Avon

**PUBLIC TOILETS** At recreation ground

William Shakespeare (1564–1616) is believed to have been a regular visitor to Bidford-on-Avon. The former 13th-century Falcon Inn, opposite the church, was one of his favourite taverns. He reputedly got drunk at the inn and slept it off under a crab apple tree on his way back to his home in Stratford-upon-Avon. He recounts his drinking exploits in the local villages in a rhyme that finishes '…Papish Wicksford, Beggarly Broom and Drunken Bidford'. Sadly, the old inn fell into disrepair and was subsequently renovated and turned into flats some years ago. The crab apple tree has long disappeared.

## Historic Bidford

Bidford can trace its origins back to Saxon times when it was called Byda's Ford, though Roman legions had earlier tramped the area. The ford would have been on their great Ryknild Street (see Walk 11). As you stroll back along the river bank into Bidford-on-Avon you'll enjoy a superb view of St Lawrence's Church and the mainly 15th-century Bidford Bridge. Lean on its parapet and watch the placid waters of the Avon flow by the willow beds below – this is Shakespeare country at its very best.

## A Church and a Famous Local Pub

The fine 13th-century Church of St Lawrence stands above the River Avon. Its first incumbent was Rogenus Capellanno in 1260, and inside you can see a beautiful church plate that was presented to the church in 1660 by the Duchess of Dudley. In the 19th century the village became known locally for its cockfighting, wrestling and swordsmanship, while the Bidford Morris Men, who remained as a team until recent years, performed at many of the important local events.

This walk takes you along the River Avon, passing a lovely weir at Barton where The Cottage of Content pub is a famous local drinking hole for walkers. You may wish to continue into Welford-on-Avon to see the timbered black-and-white thatched cottages that line its streets (see Walk 17). Your return is along the Heart of England Way.

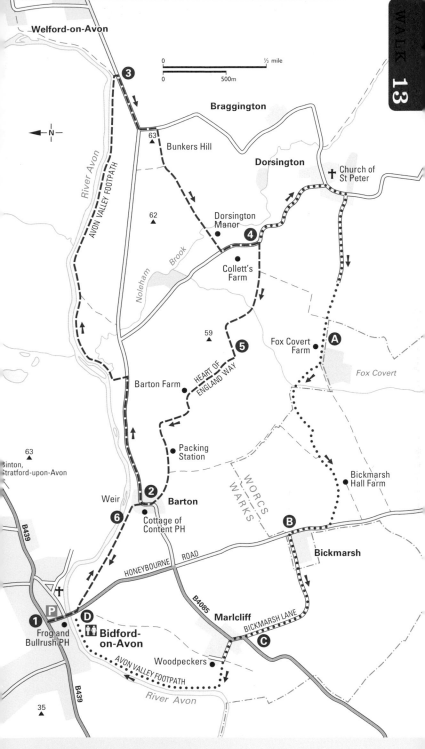

Welford-on-Avon

River Avon

❸

AVON VALLEY FOOTPATH

←N→

0 ½ mile

0 500m

Braggington

63
▲ Bunkers Hill

Dorsington

✝ Church of
St Peter

62
▲

Dorsington
Manor

Noleham Brook

❹

Collett's
Farm

59
▲

Fox Covert
Farm

Ⓐ

Fox Covert

❺

HEART OF ENGLAND WAY

Barton Farm

Packing
Station

WORCS WARKS

Bickmarsh
Hall Farm

63
▲
Binton,
Stratford-upon-Avon

❷

Weir

Barton

❻

Cottage of
Content PH

Ⓑ

Bickmarsh

B439

HONEYBOURNE ROAD

Marlcliff

B4085

BICKMARSH LANE

Ⓒ

❶
P
✝
Frog and
Bullrush PH

Ⓓ

Bidford-
on-Avon

Woodpeckers

AVON VALLEY FOOTPATH

River Avon

B439

35
▲

## WALK 13 DIRECTIONS

❶ Cross Bidford Bridge and go left through a kissing gate by a farm gate, following the Heart of England Way waymarkers through three kissing gates over a series of fields to the River Avon. Continue by the riverside until you reach a weir and lock gates, then go right up to the road in the hamlet of Barton – The Cottage of Content pub is on the right.

### WHAT TO LOOK OUT FOR

Linger in the 'Bard's villages' of Barton, Dorsington and Marlcliff (see Walk 14) and take time to enjoy the attractive cottages. Marlcliff, by the River Avon, is a delightful mix of old, thatched buildings and more modern ones that blend in perfectly. Barton boasts only a single street, but an exceptional pub, the 17th-century Cottage of Content.

❷ Leave the Heart of England Way and head left along the road for about 0.5 mile (800m). Go left through a gateway opposite Willow Cottage down to the river's edge and follow the Avon Valley Footpath by the side of the Avon for the next 1.5 miles (2.4km). Bear right to a kissing gate and climb the steps up Cress Hill until you come to a road, through a kissing gate.

❸ Turn right along the road, bearing left at the road junction by Bunkers Hill. In 125yds (114m), go right through a kissing gate and take the footpath on the right of the field hedge. This leads, via four gates and two drives, past a swimming pool, then continues over a series of fields and one gate until through a field gate you cross a footbridge over Noleham Brook, passing to the right of Dorsington Manor to reach the Dorsington

road. Go left along the road for 300yds (274m).

❹ Go right to rejoin the Heart of England Way, taking a track past Collett's Farm to a gate. Follow the waymarkers as the track crosses a stile to skirt a young copse and lake, then through a gate and over a footbridge, before following a hedge uphill. Go left and follow the path for about 250yds (229m).

### WHILE YOU'RE THERE

Climb the 700-year-old tower of Bidford's St Lawrence's Church. It rises above a small avenue of lime trees and from the top there are exceptionally fine views of the town's beautiful eight-arched bridge and the Avon, with the Cotswold Hills forming a delightful backdrop.

❺ Turn right and walk towards Barton Farm. Pass to the left of the buildings and bear left then, shortly right. Follow the track past the vegetable packing station and continue on the track as it arcs right and gently descends into Barton. At the road, go right and then ahead through a gate by The Cottage of Content pub and take the wide track down to the Avon.

❻ Walk along the riverside footpath, retracing your steps back to the car park in Bidford-on-Avon.

### WHERE TO EAT AND DRINK

The Cottage of Content at Barton is a regular stopping-off place for walkers on the Heart of England Way – children and dogs are allowed in the bar and front garden. At The Frog, along the High Street in Bidford-on-Avon, you can enjoy a pleasant bar snack by the river. Children and guide dogs (only) are welcome.

# Exploring the Bard's Villages

*Extend Walk 13 to take in several of Warwickshire's most attractive and charming villages.*
**See map and information panel for Walk 13**

See map and information panel for Walk 13

WALK 14

---

**DISTANCE** 8.5 miles (13.7km)   **MINIMUM TIME** 3hrs 30mins

**ASCENT/GRADIENT** 246ft (75m) ▲▲▲   **LEVEL OF DIFFICULTY** +++

---

## WALK 14 DIRECTIONS
## (Walk 13 option)

Leave Walk 13 at Point ❹ and continue along the road into the village of Dorsington, sparing time to walk around the village green and see the curious 18th-century Church of St Peter. Rest a while at the metal seat that encircles a lovely old oak tree by the church.

Walk past the road junction by the church for 150yds (137m), then go right up a quiet lane into open countryside. After 0.5 mile (800m), continue on a track to the left of the field hedge until you get close to Fox Covert Farm. Pass to the right of Fox Covert (Point ❹) and, where the track arcs left, cross a footbridge and stile and continue in a north-west direction. Over a footbridge arc left, then right at a wood, cross a footbridge and shortly enter the wood via a footbridge with a stile at each end. Through the wood continue until you come to the drive to Bickmarsh Hall farm.

Go left along the driveway, passing to the right of the major farm complex and on to the Honeybourne road. Go right along the grass verge of the road for about 300yds (274m),

past the roadside houses in Bickmarsh (Point ❸).

Go left along Bickmarsh Sixteen Acres Lane until you reach the B4085 on the edge of the hamlet of Marlcliff. You will pass a number of houses before reaching cultivated farmland where there is a fine view ahead of the surrounding countryside. When you descend to the road junction, go right along the B4085 for some 90yds (82m), then turn left into Marlcliff (Point ❻).

Follow the lane, The Bank, into the centre. Where the dead-end lane bends right, continue ahead, passing by a tiny thatched cottage and the corner house called 'Woodpeckers', and go down a lane towards the River Avon.

Just before reaching the river, bear right over a footbridge and through a gate and take the Avon Valley Footpath along the banks of the Avon, passing through a kissing gate and over a plank footbridge before coming to the recreation ground, via another plank footbridge. Through this you can exit on to Bidford Bridge. Go left over the bridge (Point ❹) and complete the walk by crossing the road and strolling up to the car park.

**WALK 15**

# A Natural Paradise at the Earlswood Lakes

*A pleasant walk around the famous Earlswood Lakes,
then out into the open countryside.*

DISTANCE 5.5 miles (8.8km)  MINIMUM TIME 2hr 15 min

ASCENT/GRADIENT 98ft (30m) ▲▲▲  LEVEL OF DIFFICULTY ✦✦✦

PATHS Lakeside paths and field paths, 13 stiles

LANDSCAPE Lakeland and rolling countryside

SUGGESTED MAP OS Explorer 220 Birmingham

START/FINISH Grid reference: SP 109739

DOG FRIENDLINESS Off lead on lakeside footpaths, care needed near wildfowl, otherwise under control

PARKING Earlswood Lakes (Tanworth in Arden Parish Council) car park (free)

PUBLIC TOILETS Earlswood Lakes Craft Centre

## WALK 15 DIRECTIONS

Earlswood is delightfully situated in the Forest of Arden. The village grew in the 18th century when the Birmingham to Stratford-on-Avon canal was built in 1783. In 1821 three reservoirs were completed and the village became known as Earlswood Lakes. The canal has not been in commercial use since 1936, but has developed into a major leisure facility close to Birmingham. In 1987 upgrading work was carried out to preserve the lakes for the future. Today you can enjoy the birdlife, watch the sailing boats, go fishing or stroll through the delightful countryside. There's also a craft centre here.

### WHAT TO LOOK OUT FOR

Children love the nearby Umberslade Children's Farm. Here they can get up close to the animals, including lambs, pigs, donkeys, shire horses and goats. Daily events include bottle-feeding and holding the animals, and there are trailer and tractor rides.

The walk starts from the car park opposite Warren Farm and heads towards Terry's Pool. Through a kissing gate and over a footbridge, cross the embankment path between the lakes – Terry's Pool on the left and Engine Pool to the right. At the far bank bear right to another footbridge and go left, signed Manor Farm Craft Centre, through a kissing gate and continue up a hedged path to reach Wood Lane. Go left along the side of the lane for about 400yds (366m), then left on a waymarked driveway to a campsite area on the edge of New Fallings Coppice. Walk through the campsite, passing the log cabin and, before reaching the woods, in about 50yds (46m), go right and over a small footbridge into a field. Turn left and take the path by the side of the woods up to a field corner stile. Cross it and enter the coppice. Go left and walk ahead downhill along the woodland path through the coppice. After going over a footbridge, bear quarter right uphill and, after 100-or-so paces within the edge of the wood, leave the coppice, via a well-walked path over cultivated farm land. This becomes a hedged path and leads to the road via a stile near Earlswood Station. Go right, away from the station, up the road for 200yds (183m).

Just before Kidpile Farm, go left through a hedge gap and take a waymarked footpath going north-west. Initially the path is to the left of the hedge, then enters trees through the corner of a wood via two kissing gates and a footbridge before continuing on the right, passing over a stile and through a kissing gate. It then descends to go, via a kissing gate, under a railway bridge. Continue ahead over a small stream and follow the hedged pathway along the right-hand side of Fulford Heath Golf Club. In about 150yds (137m) go left through a kissing gate and take the waymarked footpath across the golf course, following a line of small posts. The route takes you past the Golf Club maintenance yard where you bear right to a kissing gate. Through this bear left past the Club House on to the road at Tanners Green. Continue ahead, then bear right at the road junction, towards Wythall.

stile. Cross two fields via a stile and plank footbridge, eventually reaching Forshaw Heath Lane, via a gate. Go right and right again at junction to continue along Forshaw Heath Lane for about 300yds (274m), then left over the footbridge into Juggins Lane. In another 300yds (274m) turn left through Graves Coppice, exiting over a footbridge by mobile homes, to cross over the next field and go left over a stile to reach Poolhead Lane. Go left for about 100yds (91m), then right over a stile by Lodge Farm, passing farm buildings into open countryside once again. Bear half left over another stile and aim for a waymarked footbridge in the far right corner of the field. Cross the footbridge and return over the stream, via a second one, to go left along a hedge and then through a kissing gate to follow the right-hand edge of Clowes Wood.

After about 0.5 mile (800m), having gone through two kissing gates with footbridges, go through a gate and climb to the right to cross the railway line, descend left to a kissing gate and take the footpath ahead, following waymarks to stile. Continue ahead through a kissing gate and over a footbridge, then go right to emerge at the side of Terry's Pool. Continue along the path for the next 700yds (640m), then go right over a footbridge and through a kissing gate to the car park.

Follow the road for 125yds (114m) and go left down Barkers Lane. In about 250yds (229m) go left again along a footpath signed 'Forshaw Heath'. After 50yds (46m) go right over a stile to skirt a garden on a fenced path. Over the next stile cross a cultivated field to a footbridge and cross a

**WALK 16**

# Where the Wild Things Are – a Sutton Park Experience

*A longer walk visiting the largest National Nature Reserve in the West Midlands.*

| | |
|---|---|
| DISTANCE | 8 miles (12.8km) |
| MINIMUM TIME | 3hrs |
| ASCENT/GRADIENT | 230ft (70m) ▲▲▲ |
| LEVEL OF DIFFICULTY | +++ |
| PATHS | Footpaths, tracks and road in parkland |
| LANDSCAPE | Undulating parkland |
| SUGGESTED MAP | OS Explorer 220 Birmingham |
| START/FINISH | Grid reference: SP 113962 |
| DOG FRIENDLINESS | Off lead in park |
| PARKING | Visitor centre car park, Sutton Park, accessed via Town Gate |
| PUBLIC TOILETS | Visitor centre, Sutton Park |

Sutton Park comprises 2,400 acres (970ha) of wild and wooded countryside of moorland, meadows, lakes and groves and is one of the largest urban parks in the country. The ancient Roman Ryknild Street runs across one corner of the park and the Normans once hunted deer here. Shakespeare had kinsmen at Sutton and is likely to have visited the site. One of his famous characters, Sir John Falstaff, probably brought his Ragged Army here for he declared to Bardolph:

*'Get thee before to Coventry; fill me a bottle of sack; our soldiers shall march through. We'll to Sutton Coldfield tonight.'*

William Shakespeare
*King Henry IV, Part I*

## Birmingham's Lung

In 1997, English Nature designated Sutton Park a National Nature Reserve (NNR) in an effort to preserve this wonderful landscape. Although it is now surrounded on all sides by residential properties, it remains an important area for Birmingham and the local Sutton Coldfield community. It's a valuable space in an otherwise congested region and offers many leisure pursuits – for joggers, kite-fliers, cyclists and walkers. However, it is still possible to escape from the crowds and find peace and quiet.

It is the diversity of habitats in the park, which earned its NNR status. Many areas, like the heathland, wetland and ancient forest, represent habitats that were once widespread but have now completely disappeared from the rest of the West Midlands. For this reason, it is the home of a large number of resident birds, as well as providing an important stopover for migrants and other visitors. Around the pools you might see tufted duck, pochard and even snipe, especially near Longmoor Pool. It is hoped that red kites and other vanished species will one day return.

The nearby market town of Sutton Coldfield was important in the Middle Ages and owes a great deal to local benefactor John Veysey, who became bishop of Exeter in 1519. He lived at Moor Hall, north of the town and now a hotel, and built a number of notable buildings in and around the town. He also founded a school and paved the streets. Veysey is buried in Holy Trinity Church and there is a fine effigy of him on his tomb. It depicts him as a young man, even though he is reputed to have lived to the ripe old age of 103. The church also contains some interesting old brasses. In particular there is one of a Josias Bull in a gown of fur, along with small brasses of his five children. William Wilson, a mason for Sir Christopher Wren, made the marble busts of Henry Pudsey and his wife.

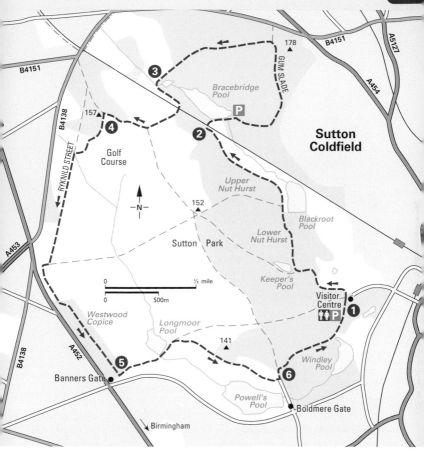

## WALK 16 DIRECTIONS

❶ Walk from the car park to the entrance road and go left and shortly right at a five-way junction to follow the tarmac lane up to Keeper's Pool. At the corner of the pool, bear right and follow the edge of the pool, then go northwards uphill through the trees on a path until you descend to reach Blackroot Pool. Walk close to the left edge of the pool for about

220yds (201m), then follow the path bearing left (north-west) and take the main track through the woodland of Upper Nut Hurst. In about 0.5 mile (800m), turn right and cross the railway bridge, via two handgates, to get to Bracebridge Pool.

❷ Turn right, along the edge of the pool, and at the end bear right along a track just before the Boathouse restaurant. Continue along the tarmac lane and through the car park until you reach a T-junction by a house. Turn left and in 150yds (137m), leave the road and go left by a large oak tree on a wide path, which soon bears right by ancient oaks in the woodland of Gum Slade. Continue ahead to a junction of paths, then go left and up to a grassy clearing. Cross it and continue ahead on a metalled track. Where this bears right continue ahead, ignoring minor cross paths, to a major path junction. Take the second left path, a metalled track, continuing ahead to a large oak tree and merging with a path from the left. Continue ahead on a track that arcs left and gently descends to cross a footbridge at the end of Bracebridge Pool.

### WHAT TO LOOK OUT FOR

The beautiful Bracebridge Pool was built for Sir Ralph Bracebridge in order to maintain a plentiful supply of fish. In 1419, he obtained a lease on the manor and chase of Sutton Coldfield from the Earl of Warwick.

**❸** Follow the track as it arcs left and then right to cross the railway line again, via two handgates. Keep on the track until you reach a road, then go right for 500yds (457m) up to a car park on the left.

**❹** At the end of the car park, go left to take the path alongside a golf green. Continue ahead through the golf course until you cross a small stream. Here turn left on to a wide, straight path flanked by silver birches. This is the Roman Ryknild Street. Continue, initially within the golf course, but later across heath, until you reach a track leading to an exit. Turn right and then left just before the exit handgate and follow the path through the trees of Westwood Coppice until you come to the car park by Banners Gate.

### WHERE TO EAT AND DRINK

There are a number of places in Sutton Park with cafés and kiosks at the various park entrances. Alternatively you could try one of the pubs in Sutton Coldfield, in particular along Chester Road North (the A452), just outside the park.

**❺** Bear left up the road, passing to the right of Longmoor Pool. About 100yds (91m) beyond the end of the pool, head right along a path. Join a path from the left and continue on it, passing to the right of a copse of silver birches. Soon you walk alongside a fence and trees, drop through a tree belt and cross an open grass area close to Powell's Pool to reach the roadway, via the left-hand car park near Boldmere Gate.

**❻** Go left at the road, then soon bear right, along the edge of Wyndley Wood, and join a tarmac lane. In 220yds (201m) bear right at a four-way lane junction on to a straight road that descends to pass a cattle grid and ford at the end of Wyndley Pool. Continue ahead to return to the visitor centre.

### WHILE YOU'RE THERE

The Wall Roman Site Baths and Museum lies 9 miles (14.5km) north of Sutton Coldfield, near Lichfield. Here you will see the excavation of the most complete public bathhouse of a Roman staging post, known as *Letocetum*. It's situated just off Watling Street, the great arterial road that connected the Roman port at Richborough, near Canterbury, with London and the north-west. Less than a mile (1.6km) away from *Letocetum*, Watling Street intersects Ryknild Street, running south-west to north-east, so this must have been a important highway junction in the Roman era.

# Black-and-White Buildings in Welford

*Explore this lovely village where traditional black-and-white thatched cottages line the streets.*

| | |
|---|---|
| **DISTANCE** 3 miles (4.8km) | **MINIMUM TIME** 1hr 15min |
| **ASCENT/GRADIENT** 49ft (15m) ▲▲▲ | **LEVEL OF DIFFICULTY** ✦✦✦ |

**PATHS** Village footpaths and field paths, no stiles

**LANDSCAPE** Residential village area

**SUGGESTED MAP** OS Explorer 205 Stratford-upon-Avon & Evesham

**START/FINISH** Grid reference: SP 148522

**DOG FRIENDLINESS** Under control at all times

**PARKING** Near The Bell Inn, Welford-on-Avon

**PUBLIC TOILETS** None en route

This walk takes you on a journey back in time – to the delightful black-and-white villages of Welford-on-Avon and Weston-on-Avon with pretty cottages and a strong connection to the Bard.

## Stunning Cottages

Picturesque Welford-on-Avon, a frequent winner of Warwickshire's best-kept village competition, was established in Saxon times by the monks of Deerhurst Abbey (near Tewkesbury, in Gloucestershire). There must be more black-and-white thatched cottages here than almost any other village in England. Three particularly stunning examples are Ten Penny Cottage, the Owl Pen and Daffodil Cottage. Welford also boasts three old pubs – The Shakespeare, The Bell Inn and The Four Alls, all of which welcome walkers. In the porch of The Four Alls is a painting that depicts four characters:

> 'The king who rules over all
> The parson who prays for all
> The soldier who fights for all
> The farmer who pays for all.'

## Maypole Tradition

Since the 14th century there has been a 65-ft (20m) high maypole on the village green. It must have been taken down some time after the Civil War, when such frivolities were made illegal, but seems to have been restored soon after. Following a lightning strike, the original wooden pole was replaced by an aluminium ship's mast. Welford is proud of its traditions and the village children still dance around the maypole in July each year.

## The Shakespeare Connection

William Shakespeare has connections with neighbouring Weston-on-Avon. John Trapp was vicar in this tiny village between 1660 and 1669. He was also a master at Stratford Grammar School for a time, and he and his wife probably knew the Shakespeare family.

53

## Shakespeare's Will

Welford's church has a register, which records the flooding of the River Avon in 1588 due to the storm that wrecked the Spanish Armada. Joseph Green, the vicar in 1735, discovered and made copies of Shakespeare's will, one of which is now held in the British Museum. In the sanctuary of the church two fighting men are depicted in full armour. Sir John Greville, of nearby Milcote Manor, is shown with his head resting on a horned sheep and flowers at his feet, while his son, who fought in the Battle of the Spurs in 1513, wears an heraldic coat with his hands in prayer.

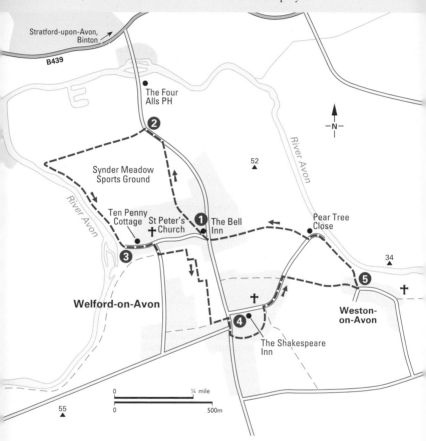

## WALK 17 DIRECTIONS

❶ Leave The Bell Inn car park, come out on to the main road in Welford and go left down the footpath at the side of the parking area. At the end of the path, near Daffodil Cottage, go right along a footpath past the back of some houses and through a kissing gate until you come to the end of Church Lane, by Applegarth

House. Continue through the gate and follow a green path at the back of more houses to reach the main road again, then go left along the pavement for about 100yds (91m).

❷ Go left again into the entrance gate of Synder Meadow Sports Ground. Walk along the track, then through a kissing gate into the sports ground and soon out

# WELFORD-ON-AVON

via a gate to continue along the footpath down to the River Avon. At the river, go left and follow the bank for 500yds (457m).

## WHERE TO EAT AND DRINK

There are three pubs in Welford-upon-Avon. The Bell Inn, at the start, is colourful with flowers during the summer months. The Shakespeare Inn lies just beyond the maypole in Chapel Street and The Four Alls is close to the weir and Welford Bridge. They can all get very busy during the summer when many visitors come to admire the flower-adorned village.

**3** Go through the kissing gate and over a footbridge at the end of the field and left up Boat Lane, lined with beautiful old thatched black-and-white cottages. Look out for Ten Penny Cottage. Near the top of the lane is St Peter's Church; go right here along Headland Road. When you are opposite Mill Lane, turn left along a footpath at the back of houses. After a kissing gate you will pass by the extension to the graveyard of St Peter's Church and continue to a junction of paths. Keep ahead here and at the next junction, go left and, through a kissing gate, walk up to the High Street to emerge opposite the Maypole Wine Stores, near the famous maypole.

## WHAT TO LOOK OUT FOR

If time permits, visit the neighbouring village of Binton to see the memorial to Captain Robert Falcon Scott. The famous explorer, whose brother-in-law, Lloyd Bruce, was the vicar in Binton, spent some time here before his expedition to the South Pole. Binton commemorated the exploits of the great man in the church's west window.

**4** Turn right along the pavement for 100 paces, then cross over and go down another waymarked footpath, past more beautiful thatched cottages and through a kissing gate. Walk through Pool Close to Chapel Street (the chapel is on the left). Go right along Chapel Street, then right again through a kissing gate along a footpath opposite to Millers Close and through a kissing gate towards Weston-on-Avon.

## WHILE YOU'RE THERE

St Peter's Church in Welford has a Saxon font bowl and carved wooden screen dedicated to the 'Fallen of the First World War'. In nearby Weston's 15th-century church you can find out about the 'Wicked Loddy'. Was he really the notorious Lodvic Greville, son of Sir Edward Greville of Milcote Manor, pressed to death with stones in 1589 for murder?

**5** At the crossroads keep ahead to descend a bridlepath set just above the River Avon. Follow it as it arcs left to come out on Duck Lane by another superb thatched house called Pear Tree Close. At the next residential drive, go right up the hedged path and walk up to High Street, where you will emerge at the junction with Church Street. The Bell Inn is on the right.

# Henley and the Stratford-upon-Avon Canal

*A gentle walk around picturesque Henley-in-Arden,*
*The Mount and the Stratford-upon-Avon Canal.*

| | |
|---|---|
| **DISTANCE** 5.5 miles (8.8km) | **MINIMUM TIME** 2hrs |
| **ASCENT/GRADIENT** 180ft (55m) ▲▲▲ | **LEVEL OF DIFFICULTY** ✚✚✚ |
| **PATHS** Field paths, farm tracks and tow path, 6 stiles | |
| **LANDSCAPE** Rolling countryside | |
| **SUGGESTED MAP** OS Explorer 220 Birmingham | |
| **START/FINISH** Grid reference: SP 152658 | |
| **DOG FRIENDLINESS** Off lead along tow path, otherwise under control | |
| **PARKING** Prince Harry Road car park, Henley-in-Arden | |
| **PUBLIC TOILETS** Station Road, Henley-in-Arden | |

Henley-in-Arden has a superb mile (1.6km) long street which offers a glimpse of the medieval world. It is lined with mostly 15th-, 16th- and 17th-century timber-framed buildings, with roofs at every level, ancient windows and a wide variety of old doors. It has often been described as a museum of English domestic architecture. The church tower dominates the middle of the town and the impressive crest on the timbered walls of the 15th-century Guildhall will catch the eye.

## Lord of the Manor

Peter de Montfort was Henley's Lord of the Manor until he fell in battle on Evesham Field in 1265. Following the battle, the town was burnt to the ground, but a new Henley rose from the ashes. The town maintains a Court Leet that has jurisdiction over petty offences and civil affairs. While this has been abolished in most towns, the Henley-in-Arden Court Leet has survived and each year the Burgesses elect a High and Low Bailiff, a Mace Bearer, a Constable, an Ale Taster, two Brook Lookers, a Butter Weigher and two Affearors (assessors). These ceremonial roles were dying out by the early 20th century, but were revived in 1915 by the Lord of the Manor, W J Fieldhouse. His title was later bought by the Pittsburgh millionaire Joseph Hardy, who established a charitable trust which now runs the heritage centre in the town.

## Memorials

Peter de Montfort lived at the castle that used to stand behind Beaudesert Church, and the hill is known locally as The Mount in his memory. The church has a memorial tablet to the Revd Richard Jago, father of the esteemed poet Richard Jago.

In medieval days the horse ruled the world of transport and coaching inns became a feature of many towns. Three very old inns remain in Henley – the Three Tuns, the Blue Bell and the White Swan. The White Swan is opposite the Guildhall and was a haunt of local poets, possibly even Shakespeare. It is thought that the 18th-century poet William Shenstone wrote the following elegant piece of verse here:

*'Whoe'er has travelled life's dull round,*
*Wheree'er his journey may have been*
*Must sigh to think he still has found*
*His warmest welcome at an inn.'*

This fine walk takes you over the top of The Mount for a fine view over Henley-in-Arden and then descends on country lanes past Preston Bagot Manor House on the way to the Stratford-upon-Avon Canal.

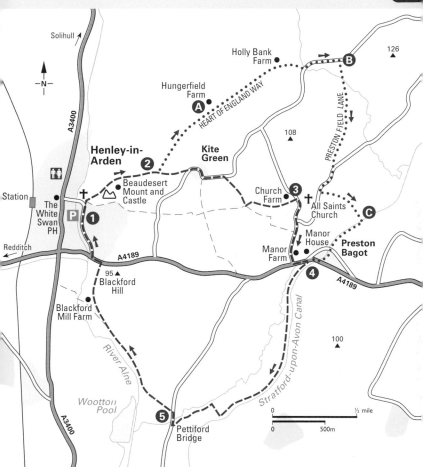

## WALK 18 DIRECTIONS

❶ After leaving the car park at the rear, walk through the gardens, cross the footbridge and go left into Alne Close. At the end you come to Beaudesert Lane, opposite Beaudesert Church. Go right through the kissing gate to the right of churchyard and follow the pleasant Heart of England Way for a steep but short ascent to the top of The Mount. Continue over the old earthworks of the former castle of the de Montfort family until you reach the corner of the top far field. Go right over the stile and continue along the footpath that runs to the right of the hedge.

**WALK 18**

**2** In about 220yds (201m), go left over a stile and diagonally cross the next field to a stile on to a lane in Kite Green. Go left along the lane for about 0.25 mile (400m), then, just past Barn View, turn right through a handgate and shortly over a stile on to a footpath that follows the left-hand edge of a field. At end of the field cross two stiles and proceed in an easterly direction towards Church Farm.

### WHERE TO EAT AND DRINK

There are a number of good pubs in Henley-in-Arden. Why not try one of the three superb old coaching inns? The White Swan, a restored 16th-century coaching inn opposite the Guildhall, is a regular stop-off for walkers completing the 100-mile (161km) Heart of England Way that passes through its archway. Well-behaved children and dogs are welcome in the bar and the large, rear gardens.

**3** After three kissing gates, go through the gate to the right of the farm buildings on to a lane. Turn right and follow the lane, passing by Manor Farm to reach the A4189 Henley to Warwick road. Go left along the road for about 220yds (201m), then cross it.

**4** Immediately before the canal bridge, descend on to the tow path of the Stratford-upon-Avon Canal, via two gates, and take this back towards Henley-in-Arden.

### WHAT TO LOOK OUT FOR

Make a short detour to see the Norman All Saints Church in Preston Bagot. Enjoy the fine view from the seat by the church which carries the message 'Rest and be thankful'. On a summer's day the altar cross becomes ablaze with light as the sun sets behind the hills to the west.

Continue past canal bridge No 49. Leave the canal at bridge No 50 and go right along lane. In 180yds (165m), this bends sharp left, bringing you to a road near the Pettiford Bridge. Turn right over the bridge.

**5** In 50yds (46m), go left through a kissing gate into pastureland. The path arcs right, diagonally over a field. Over a plank footbridge and through a kissing gate in the far corner, you reach the banks of the River Alne. Take the riverside path then, at a hedge gap junction, bear right and shortly take the right-hand footpath and proceed ahead, passing to the right of Blackford Mill Farm buildings via a kissing gate and a handgate. Continue on field paths to the left of Blackford Hill to reach the A4189 road in Henley-in-Arden via a kissing gate. Cross the road going left, then right on to Prince Harry Road which leads back to the car park.

### WHILE YOU'RE THERE

The Stratford-upon-Avon Canal was completed in 1816 to link up with the Worcester and Birmingham Canal at King's Norton. It became derelict, but was saved by a group of canal enthusiasts and has since become a fine leisure facility for boaters, walkers, anglers, canoeists and artists. Note the cast-iron split bridges on the Stratford-upon-Avon Canal – there are not many of these in the country.

# To Preston Field Lane

*A longer walk along the Heart of England Way.*
**See map and information panel for Walk 18**

| DISTANCE 7 miles (11.3km) | MINIMUM TIME 3 hrs |
|---|---|

**ASCENT/GRADIENT** 230ft (70m) ▲▲▲    **LEVEL OF DIFFICULTY** ✦✦✦

## WALK 19 DIRECTIONS (Walk 18 option)

At Point ❷ on Walk 18 continue ahead to stay on the Heart of England Way. After a 0.25 mile (400m), go right over a stile and cross the next field diagonally to a further stile. Cross this, and go left up a hedged track for 50yds (46m), then right to walk in a north-easterly direction. Go over a farm track with Hungerfield Farm on your left (Point ❹), then continue through two more fields via a kissing gate.

Through a second kissing gate descend towards Holly Bank Farm, passing to its right to reach the Henley to Lowsonford road, via another kissing gate, and a gate. Go left along the road for about 0.25 mile (400m), then turn right at Willowbrook Barn on to an unclassified county road (Point ❸).

This is Preston Field Lane and, after crossing a ford, the track becomes a green lane and then a tarmac road. You will pass a beautiful thatched cottage just before you reach Rookery Lane. Go right along the lane towards Preston Bagot. In about 220yds (201m), go left through a kissing gate opposite Preston Bagot church, enjoying the fine view as you descend fields. The route takes you through a hedge gap and then continues in a south-easterly direction alongside the right hand hedge to a gate and a footbridge. Go over the footbridge and take a footpath through the trees to reach the tow path of the Stratford-upon-Avon Canal (Point ❹).

The Stratford-upon-Avon Canal was completed in 1816 (see While You're There, Walk 18). In those pioneering days of the Industrial Revolution, canals were a major transport facility and agricultural goods and limestone were regularly carried by barge to Birmingham. In 1850 the Great Western Railway Company purchased the canal and and all its assets. As a result it gradually became derelict and eventually unnavigable. The National Trust took up a lease on the canal and, following a huge restoration programme, it was finally re-opened by British Waterways in 1964.

Cross the bridge and proceed right along the tow path towards Henley-in-Arden, taking time to appreciate the fine, old, cast-iron split bridges which were built in two halves with a gap to allow through a towing rope pulled by the horses. Rejoin Walk 18 at the next lock gate by the A4189 (near Point ❹).

WALK 20

# Brueton Park and the Grand Union Canal

*A pleasant walk in preserved parkland and along the tow path of the Grand Union Canal.*

DISTANCE 7 miles (11.3km)   MINIMUM TIME 3 hrs

ASCENT/GRADIENT 33ft (10m) ▲▲▲   LEVEL OF DIFFICULTY +++

PATHS Field footpaths and tow paths, 18 stiles

LANDSCAPE Parkland, canalside and residential areas

SUGGESTED MAP OS Explorer 220 Birmingham

START/FINISH Grid reference: SP 162789

DOG FRIENDLINESS Off lead along tow path, otherwise under control

PARKING Brueton Park car park

PUBLIC TOILETS At car park

## WALK 20 DIRECTIONS

Leave Brueton Park car park via the exit drive. Bear left into Warwick Road cul-de-sac and, at the end, cross the B4025, to the left of the roundabout. Then follow the path beside Colwell Lodge and into Marsh Lane and continue until you reach a small roundabout. Turn right here and follow Avenbury Drive. Just before you reach the first house on the right, No 16, go right through a kissing gate. Cross the busy A41 and, through another kissing gate, go into open countryside and take the path to the right of the field hedge, via another kissing gate and a stile. Follow this path over several fields, then bear right through a kissing gate into woodland. Take the path

through the trees via another kissing gate. Pass farm buildings crossing two stiles and then leave through a kissing gate. Continue ahead across a paddock via two stiles and go ahead over Ravenshaw Lane. Continue ahead through a kissing gate, walking to the right of the field hedge over several fields and through two further kissing gates, then bear left through a further kissing gate on to a stone track that leads up to the Canal.

Cross the bridge and descend to the canal tow path and go left. Continue beneath the M42 motorway and Barston Lane and exit at the next canal bridge, No 75, via a stile. Cross the bridge and a stile on to a footpath going south-west towards Grove Farm. Just past the farm complex go through kissing gate and along an access drive. Then shortly go left over a stile, then another to follow a footpath and lanes, passing attractive houses on the outskirts of Knowle. After a hand gate the waymarked footpath soon crosses a cul-de-sac to regain the path beyond No 15. At the timber-

### WHILE YOU'RE THERE

Solihull's High Street still contains some features of Tudor England. St Alphege Church has a rare altar stone in the crypt and a brass portrait of William Hill (1549), along with his two wives, Isabel and Agnes, and three groups of 18 children!

framed Keepers Cottage, bear right on a lane that leads to the A4141 Warwick Road. Cross over the road and continue ahead on a public footpath that leads over Copt Heath Golf Course towards Longdon Hall.

At the footpath junction by the golf course maintenance yard, go right to pass Longdon Hall and walk alongside a hedge until you come to the main golf course. Continue ahead over the golf course in a north-westerly direction taking care not to interrupt the golfers. Go through a kissing gate on to Lady Byron Lane.

Go left and follow the verge of the lane for about 0.25 mile (400m). Bear right into Browns Lane and in 100yds (91m) go right and walk along the verge of Smiths Lane. After about 325yds (297m), go right again over a stile and plank footbridge into initially a garden, then over another stile into farmland and continue ahead in a north-westerly direction, keeping to the right edge of two fields via another stile until you reach and cross a footbridge over the M42 motorway via two stiles. Continue ahead over a stile and a footbridge over the River Blythe. Cross to another stile and follow the fenced footpath, keeping ahead along the right-hand side of the field. Go to the right of an iron fence and over the stile on to Lovelace Avenue. Turn left and cross over Widney Manor Road into Widney Lane. Go beneath the railway bridge and in about 220yds (201m), turn right

**WALK 20**

up the Alderminster Road then left into Libbards Way.

After 350yds (320m), go right into Fielding Lane and join the Solihull Way heading generally north-east. Pass Hillfield Hall, cross Alderminster Road  and continue ahead on Fielding Lane, which becomes a walking/cycling route free of traffic. The route goes beneath the railway bridge and becomes a road once again. You will soon reach Church Hill Road. Bear left downhill, but go right up the path beside No 57 to avoid the busy traffic areas. At the end of the path, go right to rejoin Church Hill Road. Pass St Alphege Church. Continue past the church and school, crossing New Road on a wide path between Malvern House and Cedarhurst to enter Malvern Park. Turn right immediately before reaching the ornate gate piers, passing to the right of tennis courts. Past these, bear left into the main part of Malvern Park and follow a tarmac footpath that gently arcs left around the trees until you come to Parkridge Nature Centre. Go to the right of it to reach the side of Brueton Park Lake, then go left and walk along the bank of the lake until you are back in the car park.

# Crowds Flood to Kingsbury Water Park

*A lovely stroll through old Kingsbury and around the pools of its magnificent water park.*

---

**DISTANCE** 3 miles (4.8km)   **MINIMUM TIME** 1hr 20min

**ASCENT/GRADIENT** 33ft (10m) ▲▲▲   **LEVEL OF DIFFICULTY** ✚✚✚

**PATHS** Reservoir paths and footpaths, 2 stiles

**LANDSCAPE** Reservoir parkland

**SUGGESTED MAP** OS Explorer 232 Nuneaton & Tamworth

**START/FINISH** Grid reference: SP 217962

**DOG FRIENDLINESS** Under control at all times

**PARKING** Pear Tree Avenue car park (free)

**PUBLIC TOILETS** Visitor centre in Kingsbury Water Park

---

The water park around Kingsbury was once 620 acres (251ha) of old sand and gravel pits, but today it has become a major leisure facility with more than 30 beautiful lakes and pools attracting some 200,000 visitors each year.

## Water Wonderland

A path crosses the River Tame into the water park where you can stroll around a number of the larger pools to enjoy watching a wide variety of contemporary sporting activities taking place such as sailing, windsurfing, fishing and horse-riding. There are also several hides where you can do a spot of birding.

The old village of Kingsbury sits on a small hill overlooking this wonderland of water. On this high ground is the Church of St Peter and St Paul from where you get a delightful view over the lakes. The church contains a 12th-century nave, a 14th-century tower and a 16th-century belfry. One of its old arches is incised by deep grooves in which it is believed the local bowmen used to sharpen their arrows.

Kingsbury village has been associated with many famous families over the years. In the Middle Ages the Bracebridge and Arden families were involved in a Romeo-and-Juliet-type feud when Alice Bracebridge married John Arden against the wishes of both families. John's brother's granddaughter was Mary Arden, the mother of William Shakespeare.

## Land of Peel

By the middle of the 19th century most of the land in the village was owned by Sir Robert Peel. The long-serving MP for Tamworth, one-time Prime Minister and founder of the modern police, lived at nearby Drayton Manor and was buried at Drayton Basset, a few miles up the Tame Valley. The main business of the area had been agriculture, but coal mining took over. Later sand and gravel was extracted from the land on the other side of the River Tame. Today the river divides a thriving village from the Kingsbury Water Park.

# KINGSBURY

## Hundreds in Flood

You leave the water park over Hemlingford Bridge that crosses the River Tame. This bridge was first built by public subscription in 1783 and takes its name from the Hundred of Hemlingford in which Kingsbury stands (a hundred was an old Saxon local administrative area). There used to be a toll house at one end of the original bridge, but this was demolished in 1937. On New Year's Day in 1982 the original bridge was destroyed by catastrophic floods, which swept down the Tame Valley. Flooding has been a regular feature of the area, with the water frequently rising and spreading over the flood plain between Kingsbury village and the nearby hamlet of Bodymoor Heath. Most people now live on the east side of the River Tame.

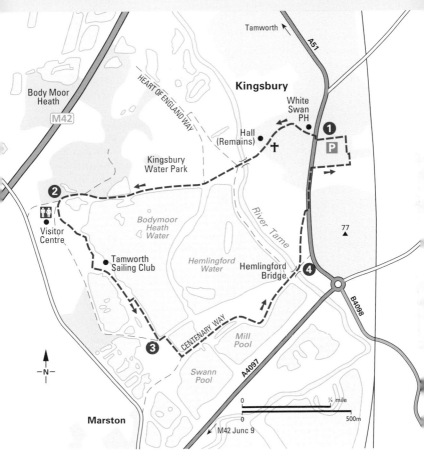

## WALK 21 DIRECTIONS

**1** From the car park, go left along Pear Tree Avenue to reach the A51 road. Go right along the pavement of the A51, then cross the road passing in front of the White Swan public house. About 35yds (32m) beyond the pub, cross over the road and go left along the well-walked footpath by the side of the churchyard. Follow the Heart of England waymarkers past the church building and descend the steps to reach a footbridge over the River

63

Tame. Cross the bridge and walk ahead along the metalled track to enter Kingsbury Water Park. With Hemlingford Water close on your left, cross the footbridge and walk by the side of Bodymoor Heath Water, leaving the Heart of England behind as you proceed ahead, eventually bearing right by a miniature railway line over a footbridge to reach the visitor centre complex.

**2** From the visitor centre, follow the signs to the watersports clubs along lanes and footpaths. Shortly the path returns to the side of Bodymoor Heath Water, then leaves it to pass by the entrance gate to Tamworth Sailing Club. Continue to the right-hand side of Bodymoor Heath Water, along a tarmac lane then back to the water's edge path.

**3** At the end of the stretch of Body Heath Water bear left, then almost immediately right and follow the waymarkers for the Centenary Way. Turning left the waymarkers take you near to Swann Pool and then, across a small car park diagonally, between Mill Pool and Hemlingford Water as your route veers in a north-east direction. Continue on the path until it merges with a lane, then keep ahead to over the Hemlingford Bridge.

**4** Immediately across the bridge, go left over a stile and cross the edge of the field to a final stile on to the pavement of the A51, near the middle of the village of Kingsbury. Go left along the pavement until you reach an area of open land on the other side of the road. At the far end cross over the road and go right, through a kissing gate, to the right of No 61, on to a clear footpath that goes along the back of some houses. In about 220yds (201m), turn left into Meadow Close, then left again into Pear Tree Avenue to return to the car park.

# Baddesley Clinton and its Medieval Manor House

*A beautiful church, fine woodland and the opportunity
to visit a superb National Trust property.*

WALK 22

**DISTANCE** 5 miles (8km)  **MINIMUM TIME** 2hrs

**ASCENT/GRADIENT** 16ft (5m) ▲▲▲  **LEVEL OF DIFFICULTY** +++

**PATHS** Field paths and woodland tracks, 1 stile

**LANDSCAPE** Rolling Warwickshire countryside

**SUGGESTED MAP** OS Explorer 221 Coventry & Warwick

**START/FINISH** Grid reference: SP 204712

**DOG FRIENDLINESS** On lead at all times

**PARKING** Lane near Baddesley Clinton Church (not church access and car park)

**PUBLIC TOILETS** None en route

This lovely walk through the heart of Warwickshire's delightful countryside provides the opportunity to visit Baddesley Clinton Manor. This National Trust property is one of the finest medieval moated manor houses in the country.

## No Change at the Manor

Baddesley Clinton Manor is the former home of the Ferrers family and its wide moat may date back to Norman times. The bridge that spans the moat is comparatively recent, being only 200 or so years old. Many of the Ferrers family were laid to rest in the nearby church. Sir Edward Ferrers, the first of some 12 generations, died in 1535. Henry Ferrers, who was born in 1549, was probably the most famous member of the family. Many people enjoyed his verse in the time of Elizabeth I and he became a notable antiquarian. The Ferrers family, staunchly loyal to the Roman Catholic faith, were persecuted throughout the 16th century by the Protestant authorities.

When Henry Ferrers let the house out in the 1590s it became a regular refuge for Jesuit priests. On one occasion as many as six were hidden in specially built priest holes, which can still be seen around the house today. The family fell on hard times again during the Civil War, when they were made to pay for their support for Charles I. Despite a few embellishments over the years, the house has seen little real change since Henry's death in 1633. It stayed in the Ferrers family until 1940, and is now owned and managed by the National Trust.

## Wren's Abbey

Nearby Wroxall Abbey was founded by Benedictine nuns in 1135. Owned and occupied by the Bourgoyne family for many years, it was purchased by the architect Sir Christopher Wren as a retreat just three years after he completed his work on St Paul's Cathedral in London in 1710. Sadly his house was replaced by the current heavy Victorian one in the 1860s. Today only St Leonard's Church and part of the cloisters remain, surrounded by glorious gardens.

# BADDESLEY CLINTON

## Heart of England Way

You start the walk from the church near Baddesley Clinton Manor and proceed through Hay Wood. The route brings you back through the splendid park of Wroxall Abbey. From the abbey parkland you continue past a converted windmill on the edge of the village of Rowington Green and join the Heart of England Way long distance footpath. Fine Warwickshire countryside and footpaths, lined with flowers in the spring, lead you back to the lane by the church.

WALK 22

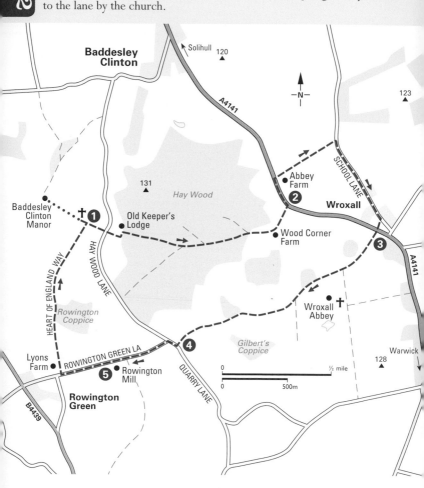

## WALK 22 DIRECTIONS

❶ From the church, walk to Hay Wood Lane. Cross the lane and walk down the track opposite, passing by the rebuilt Old Keeper's Lodge on the way into Hay Wood. Through a gate bear left for 35 paces, then right to follow the track ahead through the wood, ignoring all side paths, to emerge

via a hand gate. Cross the field to a gate between the buildings of Wood Corner Farm. Go through another gate to arrive on the farm drive, go left then right by the farmhouse and along the drive to reach the A4141.

❷ Cross the road and go left along the pavement of the A4141 for about 220yds (201m), then cross it and go right along a bridlepath between the buildings of Abbey Farm. Continue along the track until you reach School Lane and walk right along it towards the A4141. About 100yds (91m) before you reach the end of the lane, go right through a handgate and cross the corner of a field to reach the A4141 via a kissing gate near the Ducklings Day Nursery.

**3** Cross the A4141, enter Wroxall Abbey park over a stile and through a field gate, then follow the track through the grounds. Continue ahead through two kissing gates and in about 500yds (457m) the route gives you glimpses of the Victorian mansion and the old abbey building, which you can see to your left. Where the track veers left, continue ahead towards a kissing gate set in a small area of enclosed woodland, exiting from the woodland via a kissing gate. Follow this path

ahead as it goes to the right of Gilbert's Coppice and continue in a south-westerly direction to a waymark post. Continue ahead to another kissing gate before heading towards an ancient pollarded oak and following the woodland edge to a kissing gate. Through this follow the path to the left of the hedge to a field gate on to Quarry Lane.

**4** Go right along the lane, then bear left at the junction and walk along the quiet Rowington Green Lane for almost 0.5 mile (800m).

**5** Pass by the former windmill on the left and just before reaching Lyons Farm, go right through a field gate on to a track which is part of the Heart of England Way. The route takes you to the right of the farm complex, via two gates, and then along a track and through a field gate. After passing Rowington Coppice you come to a handgate. Through this, continue ahead on field paths alongside hedges, crossing the corner of a field via two handgates and a footbridge. Reaching the church driveway, turn right back to Hay Wood Lane and the car park.

# Following in the Footsteps of the Bard

*A tour of Stratford-upon-Avon, birthplace of William Shakespeare,
one of the world's greatest playwrights.*

DISTANCE 2.5 miles (4km)   MINIMUM TIME 1hr 30min

ASCENT/GRADIENT Negligible ▲▲▲   LEVEL OF DIFFICULTY +++

PATHS Riverside paths and street pavements, no stiles

LANDSCAPE Historic streets

SUGGESTED MAP OS Explorer 205 Stratford-upon-Avon & Evesham

START/FINISH Grid reference: SP 205547

DOG FRIENDLINESS On lead along streets

PARKING Recreation Ground pay-and-display car park

PUBLIC TOILETS At car park and top of Henley Street

There are other things to see in Stratford-upon-Avon, apart from the Shakespeare heritage. The medieval 14-arched Clopton Bridge forms a splendid gateway to the town. The Town Hall is a fine Palladian building and Harvard House in the High Street dates from 1596. It takes its name from the owner's daughter, Katherine Rogers, who married Robert Harvard of Southwark in London in 1605. Their son John went on to bequeath Harvard University in the USA, and the university now owns Harvard House. The Falcon Hotel was probably one of Shakespeare's regular drinking places and opposite is the ancient guildhall and an attractive row of timbered almshouses. The Canal Basin is a delightfully colourful place set in Bancroft Gardens by the River Avon.

## The Main Attraction

But it is because of William Shakespeare that visitors flock in their millions to Stratford-upon-Avon. Born here, in Henley Street, in 1564, he was baptised in Holy Trinity Church, and attended King Edward VI's Grammar School in Church Street. He married Anne Hathaway in 1582 (Walk 24 visits her cottage in Shottery) and they had three children; Susannah, Hamnet and Judith. However, a country market town was no place for a playwright and poet, so some time in the mid-1580s he headed for London. By 1592 he was the talk of the town, counting Queen Elizabeth and her court among his plays' many admirers. His poetry was first published around this time and he began to accumulate serious wealth.

By 1597 he was able to buy New Place, then one of Stratford's grandest properties, next door to Nash's House on the corner of Chapel Street and Chapel Lane. The early 1600s saw his theatre company gain a royal title (the King's Men), and the Bard, himself, wrote many of his best-known tragedies, such as *Othello*, *King Lear* and *Macbeth*.

Shakespeare began to spend less and less time in the giddy London theatre-world, and more time at home in Stratford. His son Hamnet had died, aged 11, in 1596, but the boy's sister Susannah had survived and married Dr John Hall in 1607. The couple lived in Hall's Croft, in the old

*Opposite: A view across the River Avon to Holy Trinity Church in Stratford-upon-Avon (Walk 23).*   69

WALK 23

part of the town, until after her father's death. Shakespeare died on 23 April 1616 and was buried at Holy Trinity. You can see his tomb, and that of his wife Anne Hathaway, who died in 1623. It bears the inscription:

> 'Good friend for Jesus sake forebeare
> To dig the dust encloased heare!
> Bleste be the man that spares the stones
> And curst be he that moves the bones.'

This gentle walk along the banks of the River Avon takes you past the weir and Holy Trinity Church and embraces a stroll through the town to see some of the famous buildings in Shakespeare's Stratford.

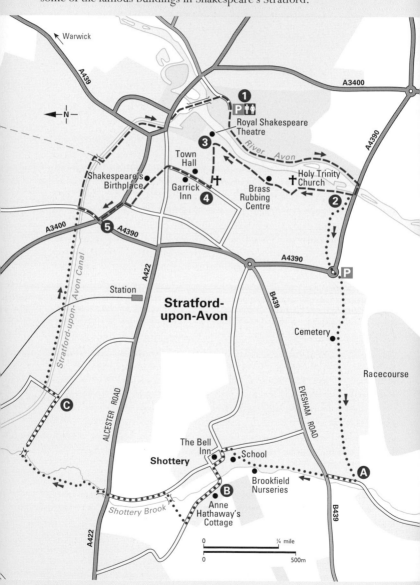

## WALK 23 DIRECTIONS

**1** From the car park, walk along the banks of the River Avon opposite the famous Royal Shakespeare Theatre. Pass the weir until you come to a footbridge over the river, just in front of the A4390 road bridge.

**2** Go right over the footbridge and bear right past the flats that replaced the old watermill into Mill Lane. Continue up Mill Lane and go through the churchyard of Holy Trinity Church, walking around the church to see the river view. Leave the churchyard through the main gate into Old Town and follow the pavement. Just before reaching the turn into Southern Lane, go right into New Place Gardens and walk up to the Brass Rubbing Centre. Continue past the ferry and stroll through the attractive Theatre Gardens by the side of the Avon, exiting into Waterside and passing by the frontage of the old theatre building.

### WHAT TO LOOK OUT FOR

Back in the 1970s and 1980s, the swans virtually disappeared from the River Avon due to poisoning by lead fishing weights. Today they have returned and together with ducks add considerable interest to the many photo opportunities available. In the canal basin, narrowboats assemble to form a colourful foreground for photographs of the Gower Memorial which depicts Shakespeare and characters from the Bard's famous plays.

**3** Go left up Chapel Lane, taking time to wander through the Knot Gardens on your way up to Chapel Street. At the top of the lane is the Guild Chapel to Shakespeare's Grammar School, with New Place Gardens to the right.

**4** Go right along Chapel Street, passing The Shakespeare and the Town Hall into High Street. Harvard House is on the left, near the black-and-white The Garrick Inn. At the end of High Street, bear left around the traffic island into Henley Street and walk along the pedestrianised area that takes you past Shakespeare's Birthplace and the Museum. At the top of Henley Street, bear right and then left into Birmingham Road. Cross the road at the pedestrian crossing and go left up to the traffic-lights.

### WHILE YOU'RE THERE

Spare time to visit some of the fantastic Shakespeare properties and indulge in the wonderful medieval atmosphere that permeates this beautiful town. This walk takes you past many attractive buildings while the longer Walk 24 gives you the opportunity to pay a visit to Anne Hathaway's beautiful thatched cottage.

**5** Head right up Clopton Road for 100yds (91m), then descend to the tow path of the Stratford-upon-Avon Canal at bridge No 66. Follow this, going south-east. Cross the canal at bridge No 68 and continue along the tow path into Bancroft Gardens by the canal basin where you will see an array of colourful narrowboats and the Royal Shakespeare Theatre. Cross the old Tram Bridge to the car park on the right.

### WHERE TO EAT AND DRINK

This short route passes the Black Swan in Southern Lane (known locally as 'The Dirty Duck') which is frequented by actors from the theatre. The half-timbered The Garrick Inn in High Street is popular with the local rugby club. The Bell in Shottery has long been used by local walking groups.

# Anne Hathaway's Famous Cottage

*A visit to the home of Shakespeare's wife in nearby Shottery.*
**See map and information panel for Walk 23**

> **DISTANCE** 5.5 miles (8.8km)  **MINIMUM TIME** 2hrs 30min
> **ASCENT/GRADIENT** Negligible ▲▲▲  **LEVEL OF DIFFICULTY** ✚✚✚

## WALK 24 DIRECTIONS
## (Walk 23 option)

Once over the footbridge at Point **2**, walk ahead up the tarmac footpath away from the river that follows the line of the A4390, then arcs right and then left. Cross over Meadowbank Road (by Avon Meadow Close) and, after a short stretch of path, continue through Old Town Mews, an estate road, to the roundabout on the A4390. By its side, cross the road with care, then proceed along the pavement into residential Wetherby Way. Follow the tarmac path to the right of No 2, soon passing the cemetery hedge and continue on a footpath through common land at the back of houses. This follows the track bed of a former railway line. At the end of the common you will come to the Luddington Road, with Stratford Racecourse entrance to the left (Point **A**).

Go sharp right along Luddington Road up to the B439 Evesham road. Cross and walk along the signed footpath opposite, by the side of Shottery Brook. Footpaths and a pavement will take you along Hogarth Road, then follow another footpath to the driveway to Brookfield Nurseries. Go right up the driveway into Shottery. At the main road, go left past Shottery St Andrew Primary School and The Bell, then left down Cottage Lane and walk up to the picturesque Anne Hathaway's Cottage (Point **B**). Continue past the cottage and in about 300yds (274m), go right on a tarmac footpath, passing several thatched cottages. You will emerge on the pavement in Church Lane where you go left up to the A422 Alcester Road.

Cross the A422 and continue up a footpath opposite, to the right of Bridge House, which meanders along the side of Shottery Brook. At the end of a grassed area, bear left and go up to a residential road. Go right, then left to join a footpath alongside the Shottery Brook. Cross a road and continue ahead, follow the left bank of the brook for 120yds (110m), then go right over a footbridge behind some swings on to the pavement of a road of industrial buildings. Follow the pavement alongside the road for some 350yds (320m), then turn left into Timothy Bridge Road (Point **C**). Cross the canal bridge and descend right to the tow path which leads back into Stratford-upon-Avon. You will pass by a number of moored narrowboats and rejoin Walk 23 by the Clopton road bridge, No 65 (Point **5**).

*Opposite: Anne Hathaway's cottage, Stratford-upon-Avon (Walk 24).*

# A Border Town with a Slice of Broadcasting History

*A short but hilly walk from Ilmington taking in some fine views over the neighbouring Cotswolds.*

WALK 25

**DISTANCE** *3 miles (4.8km)*   **MINIMUM TIME** *1hr 30min*

**ASCENT/GRADIENT** *492ft (150m)* ▲▲▲   **LEVEL OF DIFFICULTY** +++

**PATHS** *Field paths and country lane, 4 stiles*

**LANDSCAPE** *Edge of Cotswold Hills*

**SUGGESTED MAP** *OS Explorer 205 Stratford-upon-Avon & Evesham*

**START/FINISH** *Grid reference: SP 210440*

**DOG FRIENDLINESS** *On lead at all times*

**PARKING** *Sports Ground car park, Ilmington, on Mickleton Road, west of village*

**PUBLIC TOILETS** *None en route*

## WALK 25 DIRECTIONS

Remote Ilmington is the highest village in Warwickshire, standing on the border of the Cotswolds, at the boundaries of Warwickshire, Worcestershire and Gloucestershire. Brimming with typical Cotswold honey-coloured stone cottages, it is a place where time seems to have stood still. The name is probably derived from a Saxon phrase describing elms on a border hill – a mid-10th century record reveals its earlier name was Ylmandunes.

In 1934 Ilmington achieved a brief five minutes of fame when the very first Christmas broadcast by King George V was relayed to the world from Ilmington Manor, the home of the Flower family. It was introduced by 65-year-old Walton Handy, a local shepherd, and also included carols from the Ilmington Singers and bell ringing from the village. The local papers were delighted with the story, describing it as 'perhaps the most wonderful (feat) that has been accomplished since wireless has been brought to its present state of perfection.'

### WHERE TO EAT AND DRINK

The Red Lion is a favourite eating place with local walkers and reasonably priced food is the order of the day – try the excellent home-made soup. Children and guide dogs are allowed in the pub, but there is also a small rear garden. The Howard Arms, once owned by the Howard family from the nearby hamlet of Foxcote, enjoys a peaceful setting on the village green and offers delicious food and a quiet pint.

As in many country villages today, local facilities are fast disappearing. Although Ilmington still boasts a general store, a post office, a primary school and a hurdle maker, but it no longer has a blacksmith or a baker. However, it has managed to retain its two pubs – the Red Lion and the Howard Arms – and these are enthusiastically supported by local walkers. The Ilmington Morris Dancers are well known and can be seen performing regularly in the local area.

The Norman church, with its battlemented tower and fine

# ILMINGTON

Norman arches, can be seen among the trees, as can the old 17th-century gabled manor house. Inside the church is a modern sculpture of a weeping youth at an urn. It was erected in memory of Francis Canning from the manor house.

This hilly walk, by Warwickshire standards, takes you to an attractive Cotswold village, offering some of the best views in the county. Start from the village sports centre where the only sensible parking is available. Cross the sports field, taking care to avoid the playing areas. When you reach the far fence, go through a kissing gate and bear right to head towards another kissing gate. Continue in the same direction, crossing several fields and pass through another three kissing gates, but take time to pause and enjoy the fine view to the north. The path veers from one side of the hedge to the other as you descend into a valley and then, as you proceed to the top of the next rise, there is a fine Cotswold hill view with an attractive farmhouse at Lower Lark Stoke, immediately in front of you.

### WHILE YOU'RE THERE
Nearby Chipping Campden, just 5 miles (8km) south-west of Ilmington, is a typical wool town built by the affluent merchants of the 14th and 15th centuries. It has many gabled Cotswold stone houses with oriel, dormer and mullioned windows, and an outstanding market hall. A visit to this wonderful old market town is like taking a step back into the Middle Ages.

Descend to a gate near a small pool and walk by the fence on your left to emerge at a gate beside the gates of the farmhouse and on to a tarmac lane. Go left and follow this lane for about a 0.5 mile (800m). You will climb some 80yds (73m), but

stop occasionally to recover your breath and to enjoy a wonderful retrospective view over the surrounding countryside.

Just before you reach the brow of the hill and after the farm drive, go left across a field which takes you to the right of Upper Lark Stoke Farm and through a copse. Then go left again just before a gate and descend into another dell. Through a gate cross a small footbridge, go through another gate and climb again towards the hilltop. Over the brow descend to a field gate and follow the farm track, which hugs and arcs right with the contour of the hill, taking in the fine views to the left. After passing the drive to the Hill Barn, continue through a farm gate until you come to a road.

### WHAT TO LOOK OUT FOR
Crab Mill is a lovely old building, built from local stone. Earlier in the 20th century, it was home to Lady Borwick, whose fortune came from baking powder. Later it was occupied by Dorothy Crowfoot Hodgkin, who won a Nobel Prize for Chemistry in 1964 for her pioneering work in crystallography.

Do not go on to the road, but bear left to cross a stile on to a footpath now going in a general north-east direction and eventually descending towards the village of Ilmington. Just before the bottom, go left over a stile, then right alongside a hedge. The path will take you to a gate where you bear right to follow a hedged track that leads down to Hurdlers Lane in the village. At the road, go left and walk by the church as you retrace your steps past the school and across the sports area to return to the car park.

W
A
L
K

26

# An Antiquary and Shustoke Reservoir

*A stroll around the reservoir and into Church End reveals*
*changes in the landscape since Sir William Dugdale's days.*

---

**DISTANCE** 4 miles (6.4km)   **MINIMUM TIME** 1hr 45min

**ASCENT/GRADIENT** 98ft (30m) ▲▲▲   **LEVEL OF DIFFICULTY** ✦✦✦

**PATHS** Lakeside paths and field-edge footpaths, 14 stiles

**LANDSCAPE** Reservoir parkland, farmland and residential areas

**SUGGESTED MAP** OS Explorer 232 Nuneaton & Tamworth

**START/FINISH** Grid reference: SP 225909

**DOG FRIENDLINESS** Under control at all times

**PARKING** Severn Trent car park, Shustoke

**PUBLIC TOILETS** None en route

---

The beautiful Shustoke Reservoir, together with nearby Whitacre Water Works, supplies water to the bulk storage reservoirs at Coventry and Nuneaton. The reservoir is also a well-used sailing venue and is also popular with anglers and walkers.

## Ancient Scotscote

The small village of Shustoke, from which the reservoir takes its name, lies on the edge of Warwickshire. It was once a large parish, some 2,000 acres (810ha), but much of this is now under water. The village was mentioned in the Domesday survey as Scotscote, but has gone through a series of name changes over the centuries including Schustoke, Sydestoke, Shestoke, Schristoke, Sheistock and Shstooke. Its origins perhaps lie in the Saxon 'sceat' meaning 'nook' or 'corner of land'. This was once a thriving agricultural community, but much of its old way of life disappeared with the social and economic changes, which followed the Second World War.

Shustoke's most famous son is undoubtedly Sir William Dugdale (1605–86), the author of *The Antiquities of Warwickshire*. He was born at the old rectory in Shawbury Lane, the son of a Lancashire gentleman who settled in Warwickshire after marrying late in life. Today a large part of the local land is still owned by the Dugdale family.

William Dugdale was schooled at Coventry, and came back to live at Blyth Hill in Shustoke after his marriage in 1625. He was one of a group of local gentry who took up the study of local history, and it was through this that he came into contact with members of the court of Charles I. He secured a post at the College of Arms, and spent most of the Civil War in the Royalist stronghold of Oxford, where he was able to pursue his studies in the Bodleian Library. As well as Warwickshire, he focused his attention on English monastic houses.

The first volume of his *Monasticon Anglicanum* was published in 1655, two more huge volumes following in 1661 and 1673. *The Antiquities of Warwickshire*, the most detailed study of its day, was published in 1655. He also wrote a *History of St Paul's Cathedral*, published in 1658.

# SHUSTOKE

The Restoration was kind to Dugdale and he was able to continue with his heraldic work all over the country. He was appointed Garter King of Arms in 1677 and died, aged 80, in 1686. He was buried in the village.

## East and West

Shustoke is a divided village because of an outbreak of the plague in 1650. It used to surround St Cuthbert's Church, but the houses were moved to the west to get away from the contaminated site. The church, with its barrel roof and slender spire, still stands proudly on a hilltop at the eastern end of the village. In the 19th century, a bolt of lightning almost destroyed the building, but it has survived and inside you can see a monument to Sir William Dugdale.

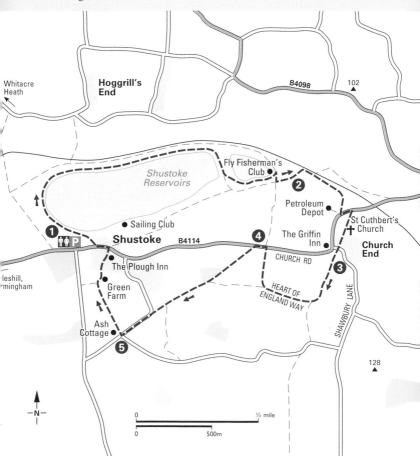

## WALK 26 DIRECTIONS

❶ Leave the car park going up to the reservoir embankment and go left to follow the fingerpost of the Circular Path which goes around the larger of the two Shustoke reservoirs. At the east end of the reservoir, go through a gate and immediately left down steps, then go right along a metalled track. Meeting a tarmac lane, go left over a footbridge, then along a path parallel to the lane which is a short distance to the south of the smaller reservoir to protect you from the possible danger of fly fishing lines. After passing behind the buildings of the Fly Fisherman's Club, leave the reservoir complex over a stile and go right along a path in woodland and cross a footbridge.

❷ Emerge from the trees via a stile and turn left to walk along the field edge to a stile and continue along a field edge, the railway on your left, before curving up to the B4114 at the entrance to a petroleum depot. Turn left along the road edge for 80yds (73m), then cross the road and go through a kissing gate into the pasture below St Cuthbert's Church. Walk half right up the field and go through a second kissing gate to the right-hand side of the churchyard and take the lane past the church to Shawbury Lane.

❸ Cross the lane and then go over a stile, situated a little to the right, into the field opposite, following the direction of the waymarkers across two fields, via one stile, until you meet up with the Heart of England Way. Do not cross the stile but go right to a stile in the field corner and follow the Way around the next two fields, bearing right at the end of the larger field to walk up to Church Road, via two stiles and, through a gate. Go left along it for 50yds (46m).

❹ At the end of a small row of cottages, turn left again over a stile to cross the field half right to a stile and take the public footpath through a small copse and then continue ahead by the side of the hedge until, crossing a stile, you come to a farm track that leads to the corner of a lane. Over another stile, continue ahead along the lane.

❺ Just before you reach Ash Cottage, go right through a kissing gate and follow the footpath across a cultivated field to a stile to the left of Green Farm. A final stile to the right of Greenacre (cottage) leads into a lane. Continue ahead and you soon reach The Green in Shustoke, close to the Plough and at the side of the B4114 (Coleshill Road). Go left, then right into the Severn Trent car park.

# Enjoying the Beauty of Berkswell

*A walk in the beautiful countryside surrounding
the ancient parish of Berkswell.*

---

**DISTANCE** *5 miles (8km)*  **MINIMUM TIME** *2hrs*

**ASCENT/GRADIENT** *115ft (35m)* ▲▲▲  **LEVEL OF DIFFICULTY** +++

**PATHS** *Field paths and parkland footpaths, 6 stiles*

**LANDSCAPE** *Gentle rolling farmland and parkland*

**SUGGESTED MAP** *OS Explorer 221 Coventry & Warwick*

**START/FINISH** *Grid reference: SP 244791*

**DOG FRIENDLINESS** *Off lead through Sixteen Acre Wood,
otherwise under strict control*

**PARKING** *Free car park near church in Berkswell*

**PUBLIC TOILETS** *None en route*

---

There are few nicer places to visit in Warwickshire than Berkswell, with its red-roofed, white-timbered cottages, the beautiful church, intriguing five-holed stocks and two historic pubs.

## Ancient Well Town

The old Saxon village was mentioned in the Domesday Book and has been variously called Berchewelle, Berkeswelle, Bercleswelle and finally Berkswell. It is believed that the village took its name from the 16-ft (4.8m), square well that is situated behind the almshouses. The 12th-century Church of St John the Baptist displays a wonderful two-storeyed, gabled and timbered porch which dates from the 16th century. Inside this lovely building is an old crypt conceivably dating from Saxon times, some 800-year-old stone seats along the walls, a Russian flag which was brought home from the Crimean War and magnificent choir stalls decorated with poppy heads and the figures of three saints – Wulfstan, Dunstan and Chad.

Although the nearby five-holed stocks were probably originally built with six holes, it is more fun to believe the local legend that they were specially made to accommodate a one-legged man and his two drunken companions.

## War Links

There is a 16th-century pub in the village – The Bear Inn. The Bear has often been described as 'the perfect example of the old English Inn', and the fine half-timbered building was once part of the Berkswell Estate and carried the coat of arms of the Earls of Warwick. It has links with the Civil War – some of Cromwell's troops were stationed at Berkswell and would have undoubtedly rested and drunk here.

A 19th-century Russian cannon, which was captured during the Crimean War in 1855 by Captain Arthur Eardley-Wilmot, the lord of the manor, stands on the front terrace of the inn. It was last fired in 1897 to mark the Diamond Jubilee of Queen Victoria. Apparently several windows in the village were shattered by the noise.

WALK 27

## Berkswell Hall

Set in beautiful farmland on the far side of the lake is Berkswell Hall, once the family home of the Eardley-Wilmots. John Eardley-Wilmot went to school with the English writer, biographer and critic Dr Samuel Johnson in the 1720s. The hall has now been converted into private residential apartments.

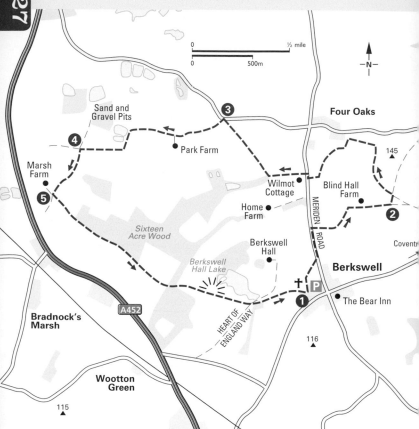

## WALK 27 DIRECTIONS

❶ From the car park go right on to Church Lane and, just past the school but before the church in Berkswell, go right through a kissing gate to follow the Heart of England Way to Meriden Road via four kissing gates. Go left along the road for 300yds (274m), having crossed to the pavement on the opposite side. Go right up a farm lane, passing through a kissing gate by a cattle grid and then Blind Hall Farm.

❷ At the end of the lane/track go through a kissing gate by the farm gate, bear sharp left and walk along the field edge to its left corner, just past a small pond. Go left over a footbridge and then through a kissing gate and continue by the left-hand side of the hedge. The waymarked footpath weaves in and out of the hedge. After continuing ahead through a wide hedge gap, walk to the field corner and go left skirting a small pond until you come to a kissing gate by some houses in Four Oaks. Ignore the kissing gate and bear left. In 90 paces go right over a plank footbridge and stile to cross the large cultivated field diagonally and exit on to Meriden Road via a kissing gate. Cross the road and continue down the driveway to the right of Wilmot Cottage opposite, going through a gateway on to farmland. The path goes to the right of the hedge for two fields, crossing one stile, offering a clear view of Home Farm to the left, then, over another stile, crosses a third field diagonally. In about 625yds (571m), through a smaller field, you will reach the corner of Mercote Hall Lane via a kissing gate.

3 Go left along the Mercote Hall Lane for about 0.5 mile (800m), passing the Park Farm complex. Walk along the lane past the large enclosed sand and gravel pit.

4 At the end of the pit area, at a track junction, go left along a footpath to the left of a copse, then right over a footbridge and stile. Cross to a gate and

footbridge, ascend to a kissing gate and walk to the left of a hedge on the approach to Marsh Farm.

5 Just beyond the farm, turn left and follow the farm track alongside the hedge towards Sixteen Acre Wood. Cross the stile into the wood and take the track along the wood edge for some 700yds (640m). Emerging from the woodland join the footpath for two fields, the hedge on your left, then go through a strip of trees into former parkland via a kissing gate. Follow the path quarter left across the cultivated field for some 650yds (594m) and you will enjoy a magnificent view of Berkswell Hall Lake before entering trees and going left through a kissing gate to rejoin the Heart of England Way. Cross the footbridge on to a planked causeway with Berkswell Hall to your left. Over a stile continue ahead to a kissing gate. Continue through a tree belt to a kissing gate and then a gate and back into Berkswell. Go through the church yard to return to the car park.

*Overleaf: A huge tree in the grounds of Berkswell Hall. The building dates from c.1815 (Walk 27).*

# All Footpaths Lead to Ettington

*A lovely stretch of open countryside with fine views.*

---

**DISTANCE** 6 miles (9.7km) **MINIMUM TIME** 2hrs

**ASCENT/GRADIENT** 345ft (105m) ▲▲▲ **LEVEL OF DIFFICULTY** ✦✦✦

**PATHS** Field paths, farm tracks and country lanes, 1 stile

**LANDSCAPE** Gentle rolling countryside

**SUGGESTED MAP** OS Explorer 205 Stratford-upon-Avon & Evesham

**START/FINISH** Grid reference: SP 251518

**DOG FRIENDLINESS** On lead at all times

**PARKING** Large lay-by at Long Hill in Blue Lane

**PUBLIC TOILETS** None en route

---

E very road east of Stratford-upon-Avon appears to lead to Ettington, a small village that is bypassed by most people on their way to Banbury or Stratford. If you stop here, however, you will discover a lively place at the junction of two former turnpike roads.

## Tale of Two Villages

Originally there were two villages – Upper Eatington and Lower Eatington, separated by a 1.5-mile (2.4km) gap. The Shirley family lived in the impressive high Victorian manor house in Lower Eatington for many years. At the end of the 18th century they decided to landscape their estate with the result that the village disappeared leaving just their house and the church, which became the family chapel.

## Three Churches

The family then gave land to Upper Eatington village and a new (second) church, the Church of St Thomas à Becket, was built in 1798. At roughly the same time Upper Eatington was renamed Ettington and the former Lower Eatington became part of the parish of Ettington.

The manor house is now the prestigious Ettington Park Hotel, but its chapel has become a ruin. Unfortunately the Church of St Thomas à Becket was built of poor quality materials and it quickly fell into disrepair. The tower, which has become part of a residential property and a local landmark at the entrance to Ettington village, is all that remains. In 1903, the Church of Holy Trinity and St Thomas of Canterbury was funded by public subscription.

## A Very English Scene

The walk starts from a lay-by on the Loxley Road, a mile (1.6km) or so out of the village, and follows a farm track towards Ettington. After passing the two Ettington churches it ascends into open countryside along a lovely stretch of footpath with fine views. The walk is completed with a stroll back up a quiet country lane.

Loxley

0 ——— ½ mile
0 ——— 500m

Stratford-upon-Avon

**1**

P

▲129
Long
Hill

BLUE LANE

Blue Lane
Farm

127 ▲

● Ettingley
Farm

A429

–N–

Goldicote
● Business
Park

**5**

Whitfield
Farm

92 ▲

DISMANTLED RAILWAY

**2**

Former Railway
Station

Nut
Wood

131 ▲

**A**

Stokeleys
Coppice

Boundary
Covert

**4**

Grove Farm

**3**

St Thomas
à Beckett Tower

**Ettington**

B4455

Ettington
Grove

Sotshole
Coppice

**B**

Rookery
Farm

The
White
Horse PH

The Chequers
Inn
●
▲
117

A429

Ettington
● Park Hotel

A422

## WALK 28 DIRECTIONS

**1** From the lay-by at Long
Hill, walk up the lane towards
Loxley. In about 0.5 mile (800m)
go right up the lane, signed
Highfield House and Ettingley
Farm. Continue ahead to the right
of Ettingley Farm, now a track.

Through a field gate continue
ahead across a field to a gate in the
hedge. Descend across next field
and, at a path junction, go ahead
over a stile to join the path to the
right of the hedge and pass to the
right of Whitfield Farm. Through
a kissing gate join the farm drive
and follow it down to the A429.

WALK 28

❷ Go right along the right-hand grass verge of the A429 towards Ettington, then in about 600yds (549m) cross the busy road with care and go left through a handgate on to the old Warwick Road. Follow the traffic-free disused road up to the A422 in the village, which brings you to a crossroads opposite the Church of Holy Trinity and St Thomas of Canterbury.

❸ Go right along the A422 Banbury to Stratford-upon-Avon road, passing by the tower of St Thomas à Becket. Just before reaching the large roundabout, cross the road and follow the grass verge along the side of the A429 for 50 paces. Cross the A429, then climb the embankment opposite and go over a plank footbridge at the top and on to a farm drive. Go left along the drive, which leads to Grove Farm, taking time to enjoy the fine view to the right.

❹ Walk between the buildings of Grove Farm, then bear right along the lane/track that passes to the left of woodland. Beyond the woodland end, the track bends left and, through a kissing gate passes to the left of Boundary Covert after which the farm track becomes grass underfoot as you proceed along the ridge with fine views all around. Go right at a junction of paths and continue to the left of the covert. Go down the track past the end of Nut

### WHERE TO EAT AND DRINK

There are two pubs along the A422 Banbury road in Ettington. The Chequers Inn is a bar/restaurant at the south-eastern end of the village. The 17th-century The White Horse is near the end of Hockley Lane, where Walk 29 reaches the village. It has a selection of bar meals, and children and dogs are allowed in the pub and garden.

Wood where it soon becomes a fenced footpath and you will shortly come to the Alderminster road, near Goldicote Business Park. Cross the road, then the main A422 (take care here) and go left along the wide grass verge of the A429, past the business park entrance.

❺ In about 500yds (457m) go right and walk up Blue Lane towards Loxley, passing by Blue Lane Farm on the way back to the lay-by and your car.

### WHILE YOU'RE THERE

Honington Hall, 'the perfect English country house', lies 5 miles (8km) south of Ettington. Built in the 1680s for Sir Henry Parker, a wealthy London merchant, this fine manor house, is set in 15 acres (6ha). An octagonal saloon, said to be the only one of its kind in the country, was added in 1751. The lavish inside contains some exceptional mid-Georgian plasterwork.

### WHAT TO LOOK OUT FOR

Take a detour to see the ruins of the old church in Ettington Park and note the epitaph to Anthony of 1587 in its tower. It ends:

'As dreams do slide, as bubbles rise and fall
As flowers do fade and flourish in an hour,
As smoke doth rise and vapours vanish all
Beyond the wilt or reach of human power,
As summer's heat doth parch the withered grass,
Such is our state, so life of man doth pass.'

# Exploring the Ettington Countryside

*A longer walk into the woodland surrounding Ettington.*
**See map and information panel for Walk 28**

**DISTANCE** 8.5 *miles (13.7km)* **MINIMUM TIME** 3hrs 15min

**ASCENT/GRADIENT** 279ft (85m) ▲▲▲ **LEVEL OF DIFFICULTY** +++

## WALK 29 DIRECTIONS
### (Walk 28 option)

Leave Walk 28 at the A429 (Point ❷) and cross over the road with care, bearing right on to the driveway towards a farm complex, passing former railway station buildings, closed in 1963. Bear left past some stables (there is a waymarker to the left of them), alongside a stream, going left at stone barns on to a farm track. Continue over the dismantled railway line and after 30 paces bear right over a stream into open fields.

Now go immediately left, the stream on your left, along the side of the hedge heading generally south-east and through a hedge gap and across a gallop. In about 500yds (457m), the path arcs right away from the stream across cultivated field to go over a footbridge. Carry on ahead up the left side of Stokeyleys Coppice (Point ❹).

At the corner of the coppice, go right along the waymarked footpath, beside the coppice. Beyond the coppice, the path bears slightly right to a mid-hedge footbridge by a waymark post, then crosses the middle of a large field to another waymark post, then continue ahead alongside a hedge to go between houses in the village of Ettington. Go right along the main street of the village and, shortly after passing the former village hall and Village Store and Post Office, go left up Church Lane.

At the top of the lane you will be in Halford Road with the Church of Holy Trinity and St Thomas of Canterbury to your right. Go left then bear right into Rookery Lane. In about 300yds (274m), where the lane bends sharp left, proceed ahead over a stile. Pass to right of Rookery Farm farm buildings on a metalled track, then left at a conifer hedge to descend pasture to a stile. Cross the A429 road.

Descend the embankment to a stile and cross the field corner to another stile, then cross the next field diagonally. Go over the corner stile and continue ahead in a south-westerly direction over two cultivated fields to a country lane near Sotshole Coppice (Point ❸) via a stile and plank footbridge.

Go right along the lane for almost 200yds (183m), then turn right again over a field stile and walk to the right of the field hedge. The clear footpath leads along the left-hand edge of Ettington Grove. At the end of the grove, bear right to cross a final cultivated field, half right, until you come out near Grove Farm and rejoin Walk 28 at Point ❹. Go left along the farm track that proceeds to the left of woodland and complete the walk.

# Meriden – the Traditional Centre of England

*A pleasant woodland stroll around the Heart of England Way, which is especially delightful in the spring.*

| | |
|---|---|
| **DISTANCE** 5 miles (8km) | **MINIMUM TIME** 2hr 15min |
| **ASCENT/GRADIENT** 197ft (60m) ▲▲▲ | **LEVEL OF DIFFICULTY** +++ |

**PATHS** Field and woodland paths, 13 stiles

**LANDSCAPE** Gentle rolling countryside

**SUGGESTED MAP** OS Explorer 221 Coventry & Warwick

**START/FINISH** Grid reference: SP 251820

**DOG FRIENDLINESS** Off lead through woodland, otherwise under strict control

**PARKING** Old Road, Meriden, near Queen's Head

**PUBLIC TOILETS** None en route

## WALK 30 DIRECTIONS

This easy walk offers the opportunity to visit an historic place and walk through some of the most attractive woodland in the area. Meriden is a pleasant commuter village providing quick access to Coventry and Birmingham along the busy A45. It claims to be the centre of England and there is a cross on the village green which carries the inscription: 'This ancient wayside cross has stood in the village for some 500 years and by tradition marks the Centre of England.'

At 18th-century Forest Hall, to the west of Meriden, there is a piece of ancient turf where the Woodmen of Arden, the oldest archery society in England, holds its meetings. The turf is believed to have been undisturbed since the trees of the Forest of Arden first cast their shade over the archery butts. The society was established in 1785 and its membership is strictly limited to just 82 archers. There is also a horn here, said to have belonged to Robin Hood.

From The Queen's Head in Meriden, walk up Eaves Green Lane following the Heart of England Way and, in about 300yds (274m), ignore the left turn for Walsh Lane and continue right on Eaves Green Lane. In a further 0.25 mile (400m) go beneath the main A45 Birmingham to Coventry road and continue into the hamlet of Eaves Green.

Continue ahead at the junction on Showell Lane, and, after passing by a mobile home park, bear left over a stile on to a path that leads over meadows into woodland, via a footbridge and a kissing gate, called Meriden Shafts. Continue through the delightful woodland and leave at its north-east end via a kissing gate and go left along the track for 50 paces, then turn right into pastureland via a kissing gate. Continue ahead by the hedge-side, across three fields via a gate and a stile and on to Harvest Hill Lane in Hollyberry End via another stile.

> ## WHAT TO LOOK OUT FOR
> Cross the B4202 road and climb the hill to visit the Church of St Lawrence. From the churchyard you will be rewarded with fine views. If you stand near the ancient sundial or by the yew tree with the massive trunk you can see the city of Birmingham and the view stretches to the hills of Worcestershire, Staffordshire and Shropshire.

Go left on the lane past Ivy House Farm, the Heart of England Way leaving the route at a sharp left bend, but you continue on the lane, in total for over 0.5 mile (800m). After passing Marlbrook Hall Farm, bear right at the next road junction to follow Becks Lane. In about 275yds (251m) the lane bends right near the entrance to Becks Barn where you go to the right of the drive via a stile on to a waymarked path over pastureland. A couple of handgates lead on to a road. Cross the road and the next field on to a quiet lane via a hand gate near two large communication masts.

Continue ahead along the lane for about 350yds (320m), then go left over a stile on to a footpath to the left of Close Wood. Over a stile skirt a pond and, via a stile enter the woodland and enjoy a delightful stretch of walking. Leave Close Wood via another stile and walk along the path over cultivated land to pass left of High Ash Farm.

By a Dutch barn turn left and descend the track to a kissing gate by a field gate. Through the kissing gate bear right, descending a lane past Lodge Green Farm to reach the Fillongley road. Cross the road and continue down Lodge Green Lane opposite for about 350yds (320m).

Turn right over a stile and take the path following a line of oak trees across a large cultivated field. At the end, go over a stile to the road and turn left along Walsh Lane to cross the bridge over the A45. Immediately across the bridge go right through a handgate and take the path high above the A45. In 100yds (91m) go left through a handgate into pastureland heading for a footbridge to the right of a pond surrounded by trees. From the footbridge continue ahead up the next field to a stile at the corner.

> ## WHILE YOU'RE THERE
> The medieval cross in Meriden may not actually be the centre of England, as has been thought for over 500 years. Satellites and global positioning technology has recently identified that it is most likely to be in the middle of a farm field some 10 miles (16.1km) away but, to many people, Meriden will always remain the true centre.

Ignore the road and bear sharp left through a kissing gate to descend over several fields towards the village of Meriden, with a hedge and later a field drain on your left. Cross the drain on a footbridge and, over a stile, aim for a kissing gate to the left of a row of fairly new bungalows and go through this on to Old Road. The Queen's Head pub can be found to the left.

# Monastic Lines at Polesworth

*A visit to historic Polesworth and the Oxford Canal.*

| | |
|---|---|
| **DISTANCE** 5 miles (8km) | **MINIMUM TIME** 2hrs |

**ASCENT/GRADIENT** 115ft (35m) ▲▲▲  **LEVEL OF DIFFICULTY** ✦✦✦

**PATHS** Canal tow paths, field paths and residential areas, 4 stiles

**LANDSCAPE** Gentle rolling farmland

**SUGGESTED MAP** OS Explorer 232 Nuneaton & Tamworth

**START/FINISH** Grid reference: SK 262024

**DOG FRIENDLINESS** Off lead along tow path, otherwise under control

**PARKING** Hall Court car park (free)

**PUBLIC TOILETS** Near Fire Station, Tamworth Road, Polesworth

This trip to Polesworth allows you to experience a fragment of monastic England and to see a beautiful, ancient abbey church and vicarage. These buildings date back to AD 827 and form part of a nunnery built by Egbert, who is often claimed to have been the first Saxon King of all England. His daughter Editha was the abbess.

### Friendly Ghost

Polesworth vicarage used to be the manor house and displays some ornate chimneys. In the corner of the vicarage garden (sadly, not accessible to the public) is a fine sundial with a square cap displaying the Nethersole and Goodere coats of arms carved on its sides. The abbey's dovecote can be found tucked away behind the village library. The superb 14th-century nunnery gate now has two residential flats in its upper storey. The larger of the two is said to be haunted by a friendly ghost. Apparently this harmless apparition moves plant pots around the building.

### Squires and Pages

The influence of the local squirearchy can be seen all around Polesworth. Nearby Pooley Hall was built by Sir Thomas Cockain in 1506, although there are records of an earlier Saxon hall on the site. The stones in the walls and the beams in the roof were taken from the ancient abbey, following its dissolution. Sir Henry Goodere became lord of the manor and there are stories connecting him with Michael Drayton (1563–1631), the poet, who was born in Hartshill (see Walk 38). In his early years Drayton was a page-boy to Sir Henry at Pooley Hall and William Shakespeare is said to have been a page-boy here. Drayton was a regular companion of Shakespeare.

### Large Village

Although the population of Polesworth has expanded to more than 9,000 people today, it retains a village atmosphere with its old part largely untouched and its many public houses intact. The River Anker and the Coventry Canal offer a quick step into the countryside, although it has been many years since

local people were able to skate along these gentle backwaters. This us
be a favourite wintertime activity for villagers.

## Fields and Tow Path

The walk starts near the tourist information office and takes you over th
River Anker on to the tow path of the Coventry Canal. After the canal's
bridge No 49, you'll leave the tow path, crossing fields and lanes to the village
of Dordon, before returning along Common Lane back into Polesworth.

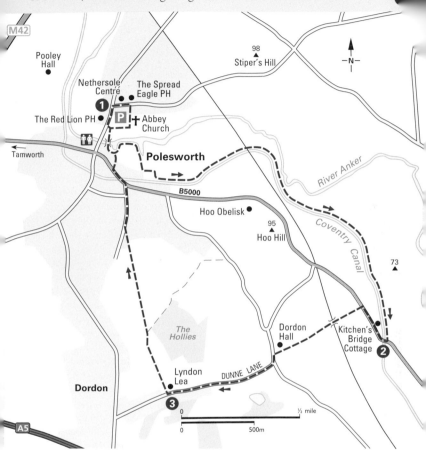

## WALK 31 DIRECTIONS

❶ From the car park at Hall Court, walk towards The Red Lion and left into Bridge Street, walking towards the bridge. After about 95 paces, turn left by the Spar shop into an alleyway that leads to a public footpath junction and turn right to take the path signed to the River Anker. Cross the footbridge over the river, then another and

bear left through the pleasant gardens keeping by the river bank on a footpath. Leave the river and head for a sports pavilion. Beyond it turn left on a path beside the bowling green that arcs gently right towards bridge No 51 over the Coventry Canal. Descend to the canal and turn left along its pleasant tow path, which you now follow for the next 1.5 miles (2.4km). You may see fishermen

to catch some of the perch,
 and chub in the canal. Before
king beneath the railway line
k up to your right and on the
 bank you will see the obelisk
n Hoo Hill. Stiper's Hill is visible
to the left. Continue beneath the
main electrified railway line.

**2** Leave the Coventry Canal's
tow path when you get to bridge
No 49 and ascend on to the road
going left over the canal bridge and
generally north-west past Kitchens
Bridge Cottage. Soon after passing
the cottage, look out for a hedge
gap on the left-hand side and
proceed through this to cross the
footbridge over the railway line
via two stiles. Now climb the hill
passing through the farm gate to
the left of the buildings of Dordon
Hall farm and continue up to the
road. Over a stile go left along
the road, then soon turn right
when you reach a road junction,
following the signpost to Dordon.
This will take you along Dunne
Lane into the village.

### WHILE YOU'RE THERE

Spare a little time to visit the
old Abbey Church and see the
13th-century stone low relief
figure that is believed to be the
effigy of the first abbess, Osanna.
She lies on the tomb of Sir
Richard Harthill with her feet on
a stag, attired in a wimple and
long straight gown with hanging
sleeves. The church tower was
built in his memory.

**3** Immediately after passing
a house called Lyndon Lea, at
the crest of the hill, turn to the
right down a track that leads to
a gate on to a footpath over open
farmland. Follow this footpath,
heading generally northwards,
towards the prominent trees of
The Hollies. Continue left past the
trees, crossing a stile and, ignoring

### WHAT TO LOOK OUT FOR

Look up to the right, midway
through Point **1**, for a close
up view of Hoo Obelisk on the
far bank of the canal. This was
originally erected in around
1848 close to the London
Railway Line on the opposite
side of the canal, but was
moved in the 20th century for
safety reasons. The inscription
reads: 'Site of the Chapel of St
Leonard at Hoo demolished
1538 30th Henry VIII'.

a kissing gate, continue ahead
along a hedged path. Soon you
will find yourself walking along a
surfaced farm track that becomes
Common Lane on the approach
to Polesworth village. Take the
pavement of the lane through a
residential estate until you reach
the B5000 Tamworth to Grendon
road. Turn left and cross the road,
with care as it can be busy, and
stroll over the canal bridge. Turn
right at Polesworth Garage down
to the park area by the River Anker
and cross back over the footbridge.
The public footpath now leads up
to a junction of paths where you
go right, towards the abbey. Bear
left and leave through the Old
Nunnery Gateway on to the High
Street. Now turn left and continue
along the High Street, past the
Nethersole Centre and turn left
again into Bridge Street to return
to Hall Court car park.

### WHERE TO EAT AND DRINK

There are several good public
houses in Polesworth and you
will pass by a number along the
route of the walk. The Spread
Eagle and The Red Lion do not
provide food but the Fosters
Yard pub on the corner of
Market Street and Grendon
Road will look after you well.
The bar snacks and Pedigree
real ale will appeal (children and
dogs welcome).

# Deer Spotting Around Charlecote

*An easy walk into open countryside,*
*but you may ask where have the deer gone?*

> **DISTANCE** 6 miles (9.7km)  **MINIMUM TIME** 2hr 15min
>
> **ASCENT/GRADIENT** 33ft (10m) ▲▲▲  **LEVEL OF DIFFICULTY** ✦✦✦
>
> **PATHS** Field paths and farm tracks, 2 stiles
>
> **LANDSCAPE** Gentle rolling countryside
>
> **SUGGESTED MAP** OS Explorer 205 Stratford-upon-Avon
>
> **START/FINISH** Grid reference: SP 263564
>
> **DOG FRIENDLINESS** Under control at all times
>
> **PARKING** National Trust visitors car park for Charlecote Park (closed at night)
>
> **PUBLIC TOILETS** None en route

This walk starts in the delightful village of Charlecote, about 5 miles (8km) from Stratford-upon-Avon. There is an opportunity to visit the superb Charlecote Park (now cared for by the National Trust), which has been the home of the Lucy family since 1247. The route passes along the banks of the pretty River Dene to the edge of the village of Wellesbourne and then crosses farmland and farm lanes on its return to Charlecote, passing close to 19th-century Charlecote Mill.

### Elizabethan Jewel

Charlecote Park house comprises an Elizabethan house that is largely hidden from the road by a fine parapeted gatehouse with an oriel window above its arch. The hall was rebuilt in 1558 by Sir Thomas Lucy, in the shape of the letter E and is surrounded by a wonderful deer park. For more than 200 years fallow deer have been bred from stock and have roamed freely in the large park. Until recently some 250 fallow deer and 150 red deer (introduced by Henry Spencer Lucy in the 1840s) shared the park. Sadly, during 2001–2, an outbreak of bovine tuberculosis disease forced the estate managers to cull the entire herd. Thirty beasts were reintroduced in November 2002 and, while numbers have increased, the 100 or so Jacob sheep currently seem to have much of the huge park to themselves.

### Bard Nicked

It was in Charlecote Park that William Shakespeare is alleged to have been arrested for deer poaching. This is often cited as being the reason for his departure from Stratford for London in the mid-1580s. The legend continues that the Bard got his own back on Sir Thomas Lucy and made him the butt of the world's laughter by depicting him as Mr Justice Shallow in his play *The Merry Wives of Windsor*. Whether there is any truth in this story is debatable. Doubters will always point to the fact the deer park had not yet been developed at Charlecote in Shakespeare's day. What is certain is that Sir Thomas Lucy was locally unpopular as a Justice of the Peace, and the subject of several mocking ballads being sung in and around the pubs of

# CHARLECOTE

Stratford at the time. Shakespeare would certainly have known of these and could easily have adopted the caricature for his play.

By the roadside on the edge of the grounds of Charlecote Park is St Leonard's Church. It stands on the site of an earlier 12th-century church which was demolished in 1849. Originally the church was part of the estate, paid for by Mrs Mary Elizabeth Lucy who laid the church's foundation stone. Inside the church is the Lucy Chapel which holds the 17th-century tombs of three Sir Thomas Lucys.

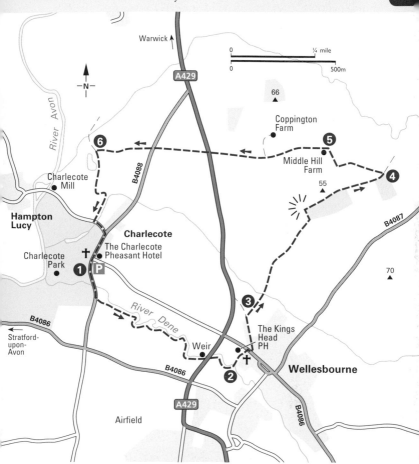

## WALK 32 DIRECTIONS

**1** From Charlecote Park car park, go left along the grass verge and cross over the River Dene. In about 100yds (91m), go left along a wide track that arcs left on to a clear fenced path by the side of the river and walk along for this about 1.5 miles (2.4km), passing a sewage farm, via a kissing gate,

into the village of Wellesbourne. You will pass a pleasant weir and go beneath the A429 before you come to a footbridge near St Peter's Church.

**2** Go left over the footbridge and up a fenced path to the left of the church until you reach the village through the churchyard gates. Continue up the road to the left

**WHERE TO EAT AND DRINK**

The Charlecote Pheasant Hotel has a fine lounge, can cater easily for large numbers and offers an excellent carvery. In Wellesbourne the walking route goes close to The Kings Head pub. Children are allowed, dogs are restricted to the gardens.

of house No 21 – The Kings Head pub is on the left – then cross the main road in the village and walk up Warwick Road opposite.

**3** In about 300yds (274m), just after passing Daniell Road, go right along a tarmac path alongside modern houses. Cross a footbridge and, go through a kissing gate, continue ahead over cultivated field. Through another kissing gate, continue ahead to cross another over a plank footbridge. Continue ahead along the left side of a hedge. Through a hedge gap take the footpath to the left of the copse of trees, then go right into the woodland. Turn left along the green lane at the top of a hedge of trees. You will emerge from the trees for a short distance and then re-enter again. After you emerge for a second time, look for a hedge gap to the left.

**4** Go through the gap and cross cultivated field to a hedge corner. Continue ahead alongside the

hedge to a field corner, then bear right to Middle Hill Farm.

**5** At a waymark post go left, between the farm buildings, then go to the right of the farmhouse and walk along the farm access lane for about 0.75 miles (1.2km), passing the entrance to Coppington Farm on the way to the A429. Cross the road with care and go over the stile opposite on to a fenced footpath. After crossing another minor road, continue ahead along a concrete driveway to skirt a brick farm building via three kissing gates.

**6** Continue ahead alongside a post and wire fence in pastureland. Bear left at a kissing gate (don't go through it) to a second kissing gate which leads into a large cultivated field that you walk around by the field hedge, initially alongside a long lake. Go right, through a further kissing gate, and continue to the right of the field hedge until you go through a final kissing gate on to Charlecote Road. Go left along the footway past a delightful thatched cottage into the centre of Charlecote, then turn right along the grass verge of the main street past the half-timbered houses and the Charlecote Pheasant Hotel, with St Leonard's Church opposite, to reach the Charlecote Park car park.

**WHILE YOU'RE THERE**

Visit Charlecote Mill and see the 19th-century mill grind corn by waterpower. There has been a mill on the site since the Norman Conquest, but the present one was built in about 1800. It stopped grinding corn by waterpower in 1939 but has since been restored. In 1983 it was acquired by the present owner and brought back into full time use. Call (01789) 842072 to confirm your visit.

**WHAT TO LOOK OUT FOR**

As well as visiting Charlecote Park, take some time to explore the village of Wellesbourne and seek out Chestnut Square in Wellesbourne Mountford and the thatched pub, the Stags Head, in a corner. A plaque in the bus shelter records that it was here, in 1872, that Joseph Arch inaugurated the first trade union for agricultural workers. The event is remembered with an annual parade.

# Warwick and the Kingmaker

*Stroll along the Grand Union Canal
and visit magnificent Warwick Castle.*

---

**DISTANCE** 5 miles (8km)   **MINIMUM TIME** 2hrs

**ASCENT/GRADIENT** 33ft (10m) ▲▲▲   **LEVEL OF DIFFICULTY** ✦✦✦

**PATHS** Canal and riverside paths, street pavements, no stiles

**LANDSCAPE** Canalside and historic town

**SUGGESTED MAP** OS Explorer 221 Coventry & Warwick

**START/FINISH** Grid reference: SP 277647

**DOG FRIENDLINESS** Off lead along tow path, otherwise under control

**PARKING** Racecourse car park (St Mary's Area 3 car park,
at north end of racecourse)

**PUBLIC TOILETS** None en route

---

This easy walk offers the opportunity to visit one of the most famous castles in England. Starting from the car park at Warwick Racecourse, a stroll along the tow path of the Grand Union Canal to the River Avon brings you to Castle Bridge. This offers a classic view of Warwick castle.

## Fortress Home

Built in the 14th century, Warwick Castle sits imperiously above the River Avon near the centre of the town. It is the ancestral home of the Earls of Warwick, of whom Richard Beauchamp (1428–71) was probably the most famous. He lived through the reigns of three kings and was present at the burning of Joan of Arc, before later dying in Rouen.

You can spend a whole day at Warwick Castle, there is so much to see: the Bailey, Guy's Tower (128ft/39m high), Caesar's Tower (147ft/45m high), the Gatehouse, the Clock Tower and the Old Bridge over the River Avon are all truly superb. Inside you can see the tapestry of the gardens of Versailles, Cromwell's helmet and Queen Anne's travelling trunk. Outside, there are gardens laid out by Lancelot 'Capability' Brown in the 18th century.

Tear yourself away from the castle to continue the walk, through the county town of 'Shakespeare Country'. It displays a fascinating blend of Georgian and Tudor architecture. In Castle Street you pass the timbered home of Thomas Oken – now housing a doll museum (see What to Look Out For). St Mary's Church is up the road opposite. You can climb its great 174ft (53m) tower for a fantastic view of the town and the surrounding countryside. Inside the church is the 15th-century Beauchamp Chapel where the body of Richard Beauchamp lies. Near by in St Mary's is the tomb of Ambrose Dudley, Earl of Leicester – it is said to have been made by the same craftspeople who modelled Shakespeare's bust at Stratford.

Before heading back to the racecourse you'll pass Lord Leycester's Hospital, at the West Gate of Warwick. This was originally the Guild House of St George which became the Almshouse in 1571 founded by Robert Dudley. Now it is probably the most famous medieval building in this fine town.

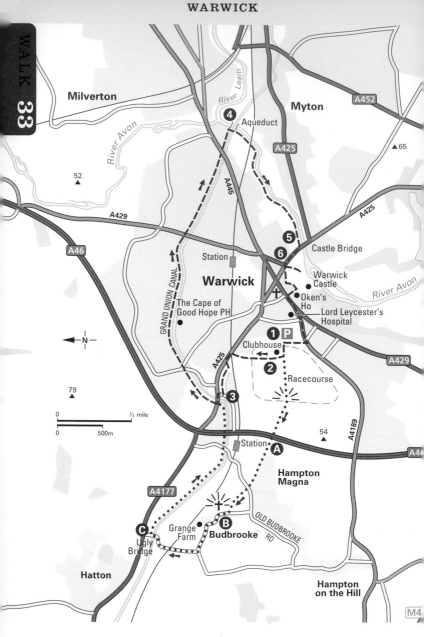

WALK 33

## WALK 33 DIRECTIONS

**1** Walk to the end of the racecourse car park and go left towards the golf clubhouse, the Warwick Golf Centre.

**2** Beyond, go right and take the wide green track between the

golf course and the driving range. In about 300yds (274m), cross over the racetrack and go through a kissing gate on to a footpath alongside modern housing. Continue ahead and, at the corner of common land, go right through a kissing gate on to a lane and descend to the road. Go left along the pavement beneath the railway bridge, then left opposite St Michael's Road through a gate on to grassland by the Saltisford Canal. Follow this grassy area to the tow path, passing a large narrowboat mooring area and climb the steps up to the canal bridge on to the pavement beside a road. Go right, along the pavement and in 50yds (46m) you will come to a canal bridge over the Grand Union Canal and the busy A425.

### WHERE TO EAT AND DRINK
There are several good eating places in the town of Warwick. Along the walk route The Cape of Good Hope by the side of the Grand Union Canal is a popular pub with walkers – children and dogs are welcomed. It has a patio overlooking the canal and serves bar snacks and good ale.

❸ Cross the road with care. Go left over the canal bridge and, immediately across it, descend to take the tow path into Warwick, about 1.5 miles (2.4km) away, passing by a lock gate with The Cape of Good Hope pub opposite and then going along the back of residential properties. Shortly after passing by a Tesco store and just before reaching the aqueduct over the River Avon, go left down steps to join the 'Waterside Walk', turning right at stream.

❹ Proceed right under the aqueduct and follow the river bank footpath. At Castle Bridge, climb steps on to the pavement of the A425 (Banbury) road and cross with care.

❺ Stroll on to the bridge for the classic view of Warwick Castle, then turn around and follow the pavement towards Warwick town.

### WHILE YOU'RE THERE
No trip to Warwick is complete without a visit to Warwick Castle, but do walk carefully as you enter the eerie Ghost Tower for you may not be alone. It was here, in 1628, that the castle's then owner, Sir Fulke Greville, was fatally stabbed by a manservant because he did not bequeath sufficient funds to him in his will. Entry to the castle isn't cheap – the castle is run on commercial lines by the Tussauds Group – but it's reasonable out of high season. It's open 10am–6pm April to September, 10am–5pm October to March.

❻ In 220yds (201m) go left and meander down picturesque Mill Street for the second classic view of the castle. Return to the main road and go left through the main entrance gate to Warwick Castle grounds. Bear right and leave the grounds via a wall gate into Castle Street, signed 'Exit to Town'. Stroll up Castle Street, passing by Oken's House until you reach the tourist information centre on the corner of the High Street. Turn left here and walk along High Street, going beneath the archway of the Lord Leycester Hotel. Go right into Bowling Green Street and, in 50yds (46m), turn left down Friars Street to reach Warwick Racecourse and the St Mary's Area 3 car park.

### WHAT TO LOOK OUT FOR
As you walk up Castle Street you pass a pretty timber-framed 15th-century house. This is Thomas Oken's House. Oken was a silk and luxury goods merchant and a famous Warwick benefactor. He founded an almshouse for poor women, endowed a schoolmaster and provided money for bonfires for the young. He was Master of the Guild at the time of the 1545 town charter.

# Budbrooke and the Warwickshire Regiment

*An opportunity to visit the home village of the Warwickshire Regiment.*
**See map and information panel for Walk 33**

> **DISTANCE** 8 miles (12.9km) **MINIMUM TIME** 3 hrs
> **ASCENT/GRADIENT** 69ft (21m) ▲▲▲ **LEVEL OF DIFFICULTY** +++

## WALK 34 DIRECTIONS (Walk 33 option)

From the golf driving range building (near Point ❷), continue ahead on the clearly waymarked footpath walking in a north-westerly direction. Before crossing the racetrack pause to enjoy a fine retrospective view over Warwick, then over the footbridge, go through a right handgate and continue across pastureland, alongside a hedge to a stile. When you reach the field hedge by the busy A46, go over a stile and through a kissing gate to cross it with care. Then, through another kissing gate, follow the footpath to the left of the field hedge, climbing towards the village of Hampton Magna (Point ❹). Over a stile the footpath takes you past a residential estate on to the Old Budbrooke Road via another stile where there is a large stone recalling the history of the Warwickshire Regiment, whose barracks were once located here at Budbrooke.

Cross the road and a footbridge, go through a kissing gate and continue over the stile opposite into meadowland. The footpath arcs right, passing a pond, then veers left through another kissing gate towards the church in the small village of Budbrooke (Point ❸). Through a kissing gate

and gate, you reach the 13th-century parish church which contains a marble monument to Rowland Dormer. Grove Park, the home of the Dormers, an influential family, is located in wooded parkland near by. From the church there is a grand view of Warwick town, with the tower of St Mary's and the castle prominent amid the trees. There are also several memorials to the fallen soldiers of the Warwickshire Regiment.

At the church car park, go right through the churchyard and through a gate on to a lane. Go right again along the lane past Grange Farm and under the railway line to reach Ugly Bridge over the Grand Union Canal (Point ❸). Pause on the bridge and look north-west up the canal to see the attractive row of Hatton Lockgates. There are 21 lockgates and the canal rises some 140ft (42m) over 2 miles (3.2km). You may be lucky enough to see a narrowboat making its way down the flight of locks. Now descend to the tow path and follow it, going south-east towards Warwick.

After passing by six lockgates, including Hatton Bottom Lock (near Warwick Parkway railway station), rejoin the main walk by the A425 at Point ❸.

*Opposite: Looking towards Warwick Castle from the River Avon (Walk 33).*

# History at Kenilworth

*Explore historic Kenilworth Castle and the surrounding countryside.*

WALK 35

| | |
|---|---|
| **DISTANCE** 4.5 miles (7.2km) or 5.5 miles (8.8km) if you visit Honiley church | |
| **MINIMUM TIME** 2hrs 15min | |
| **ASCENT/GRADIENT** 105ft (32m) ▲▲▲   **LEVEL OF DIFFICULTY** ✦✦✦ | |
| **PATHS** Field paths and farm tracks, 1 stile | |
| **LANDSCAPE** Rolling countryside | |
| **SUGGESTED MAP** OS Explorer 221 Coventry & Warwick | |
| **START/FINISH** Grid reference: SP 279723 | |
| **DOG FRIENDLINESS** On lead at all times | |
| **PARKING** In front of castle by Castle Green | |
| **PUBLIC TOILETS** None en route | |

## WALK 35 DIRECTIONS

The dramatic ruins of Kenilworth Castle are an important part of English history. This walk starts from the castle and goes over farmland, then circles around Chase Wood to return along a track from where the best views of the castle ruins can be enjoyed.

This was the stronghold for lords and kings of England in the 11th and 12th centuries. Originally it was a timber fortress and King John paid several visits to the castle, providing £2,000 for its defences.

### WHAT TO LOOK OUT FOR

If you complete this walk in the spring you can expect to see a carpet of bluebells in Chase Wood. Look out for the views of Kenilworth Castle as you complete the walk and pause from time to time at different points along the walk. After draining part of the lake around the castle, Henry V built a summer house on 'The Pleasance' – can you spot the site?

In the 14th century, John of Gaunt transformed the fortress into a grand castle, building a great hall. The castle later passed to Henry IV and remained a royal residence until Queen Elizabeth I gave it to Robert Dudley in 1563. It was then used to host a series of lavish entertainments for the Queen. The Civil War brought about its demise when, after a long siege, Cromwell ordered the defences to be dismantled. Later it was the setting for large parts of the action in Sir Walter Scott's historical novel *Kenilworth*. It is now in the hands of English Heritage.

From the car park, go through the kissing gate to the left of impressive Kenilworth Castle. Take the footpath that circles around the castle walls, including climbing over the causeway and descending to a kissing gate, then go ahead, to the left of a beautiful pink, thatched cottage, and on to a good wide track.

Go left along this track for 120yds (110m), then right through a kissing gate into a cultivated field. Follow the well-walked footpath diagonally north-west across the field. Pause at the field corner to enjoy a fine retrospective view of the castle and then leave the main path by going right, up a less-used green track going north. Walk ahead along this track over several fields and through a kissing gate until you come to Chase Lane, passing to the left of East Chase Farm.

Over a stile, head left and stroll along Chase Lane for the next 1.5 miles (2.4km). This is pleasant, easy walking passing a pair of red-brick cottages, where other paths emerge, the entrance driveway to Pleasance Farm and several attractive cottages before going to the right of Chase Wood. The wood displays a carpet of bluebells in spring. As you approach the end of the wood, the large complex of Warriors Lodge Farm is close ahead. At the wood end, go left and descend a stony farm track to the west of Chase Wood. Up to your right you can see Honiley church.

After about 400yds (366m) you reach a junction of footpaths. To Honiley there is a footpath going to the right here, which leads up to the church. It will add about a further mile (1.6km) to your walk.

Simon de Montfort, the Earl of Leicester, built his home in Honiley and obtained a licence from the Pope to build a church and to put a statue to St John and a picture

of the Blessed Virgin in it. At the beginning of the 18th century John Sanders bought Honiley and decided to rebuild the church. Legend has it that the architect Sir Christopher Wren, a neighbour who was nearing his 90th birthday at the time, sketched a design for the new church on his tablecloth and Sanders used it to build the lovely baroque building. Although the old hall was pulled down in 1820, Sanders' outbuildings remain. There are two wells (St John's Well and Our Lady's Well) near the church and pilgrims flocked to the site. Sadly there is no longer public access to the wells.

### WHILE YOU'RE THERE

Take the opportunity to visit English Heritage's Kenilworth Castle. This is England's most extensive castle ruin and is famous as the place where Henry V rested after his victory at Agincourt in 1415. A climb to the top of Saintlowe Tower is rewarded with a wonderful view.

At the junction of footpaths, go left along a fine wide grass track to the right of the field hedge with Chase Wood further to the left. Follow this straight track for about 0.5 mile (800m) going over a footbridge. After two kissing gates, continue over the Pleasance Mound earthworks to a kissing gate, then walk along the hedged footpath that leads to the farm drive to Holly Fast. Continue ahead along the drive and, as you reach the brow of the hill, another classic view of Kenilworth Castle appears. This fine prospect will follow you as you descend the other side of the hill.

Just before reaching the pink, thatched cottage, turn right on to a well-walked footpath that leads by the walls of the castle and back to your car.

### WHERE TO EAT AND DRINK

The Queen and Castle, and The Clarendon Arms by Castle Green in Kenilworth are two popular eating places where walkers congregate after a visit to the area. In the town itself there are lots of other cafés, restaurants and pubs to discover.

# Long Compton and the Rollright Stones

*An uncharacteristically steep ascent reminds you that you're now in the Cotswolds and brings you to the historic Rollright Stones.*

---

**DISTANCE** 5 miles (8km)   **MINIMUM TIME** 2 hrs

**ASCENT/GRADIENT** 673ft (205m) ▲▲▲   **LEVEL OF DIFFICULTY** ✦✦✦

**PATHS** Field paths and country lanes, 9 stiles

**LANDSCAPE** Rolling countryside on edge of Cotswold hills

**SUGGESTED MAP** OS Explorer 191 Banbury, Bicester & Chipping Norton

**START/FINISH** Grid reference: SP 308394

**DOG FRIENDLINESS** Under control at all times

**PARKING** Near The Red Lion, Long Compton (ask permission from the hotel)

**PUBLIC TOILETS** None en route

---

This short, hilly walk offers the chance to visit the Rollright Stones, set up on the hills on the county border with Oxfordshire. The walk starts from Long Compton and ascends the lane up towards Little Rollright. The route passes by the famous stones and returns over farmland into the picturesque village of Little Rollright before descending back into Long Compton. This is a pleasant village through which the A3400 winds its way between Stratford-upon-Avon and Oxford. You may be enchanted by the fine old stone houses that line the road and the unusual lychgate to the village church. This was once a 16th-century cottage from which the lower storey has been removed. It appears like a two-storey gatehouse with an arch beneath. The old church has loopholes which may have been used by marksmen during the Civil War.

## Bronze Age Stone Circle

The Rollright Stones comprise some 60 monoliths positioned in three sets. The King Stone is on the Warwickshire side of the road while the Whispering Knights and the group called the King's Men are on the other side, in Oxfordshire.

The stones, which are much older than those found at Stonehenge, are all rough worn by the winds and centuries of rain. The King Stone is the largest at nearly 9ft (2.75m) and this is said to be placed in such a position that when seen from the centre of the King's Men circle on 21 June, the rising sun is immediately in line with the stone. The stones in the King's Men circle measure from between 4ft (1.2m) to 7ft (2.1m).

## Witch Meets King

Long Compton is well known for its witches and it is not surprising that the ancient stones are surrounded by legend. The most well known of these suggests that the stones were once human – a king, his knights and their followers. The king is said to have met a witch close to where the stones stand and she told him to take seven strides to the top of the hill saying: 'If Long Compton thou canst see, King of England shalt thou be.'

## Traitors Turned to Stone

When he got to the top of the hill, he couldn't see Long Compton because a spur of land obstructed the view. The witch then turned them all to stone – the King Stone and the King's Men. The Whispering Knights are said to have been traitors who were plotting against the King.

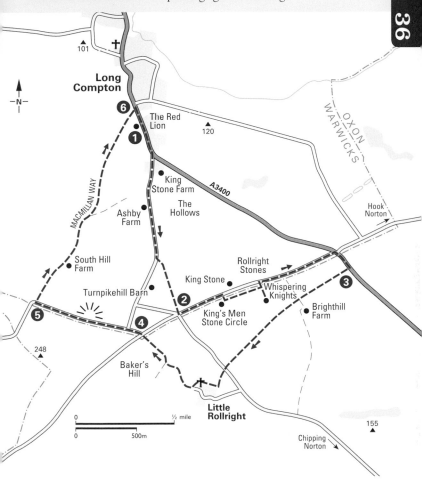

## WALK 36 DIRECTIONS

**1** From The Red Lion, go right, along the A3400 through Long Compton. Where the road bends sharp left, go right and walk up Little Rollright Road, passing King Stone Farm and Ashby Farm as you climb an area known as The Hollows. After about 0.5 mile (800m), the road bends slightly to the right and here you go left on to a footpath with Turnpikehill Barn away to your right. Ascend the footpath to the lane near to the Rollright Stones.

**2** Go left along the lane to the famous stones. In just over 0.25 mile (400m), you will find the King's Men Stone Circle on the right, with King Stone in the field on the left. After looking at the King's Men stone circle, continue along a grassy permissive path parallel to the road for a

WALK 36

further 500yds (457m), then bear right along the footpath to see the third group of stones called the Whispering Knights. Return to the road and turn right to continue along it for about another 0.5 mile (800m), then at the A3400 junction go to the right and at the brow of the hill go right again up some steps to a field.

❸ Continue ahead along a grassy path over several fields and stiles. Cross the driveway to Brighthill Farm and descend to a lane, then across it descend to Little Rollright via two kissing gates. At a lane turn right to curve north to the superb church. From the church ascend the footpath, signed 'Little Compton Footpath Only', up Baker's Hill to the road.

❹ Over a stile cross the road to follow the lane opposite for the next 0.5 mile (800m) towards Little Compton, enjoying the fine view to the right over Long Compton and towards the village of Brailes.

❺ Where the road bends left, go right over a stone stile (not straight on to the bridleway track) and down a path over a cultivated field in a generally north-east direction – the view ahead is superb. Descend to the left of South Hill Farm and continue walking on the MacMillan Way

path over several fields and stiles. The path becomes a surfaced road. Just after passing to the right of farm buildings, go left over a stile, then continue ahead by the side of the hedges of several fields down into Long Compton. Leave the footpath through a pair of farm gates to arrive back in the village.

❻ Go right, past a private house called Daddy's Bank, and return to The Red Lion car park.

# Walking Over the Hill at Brailes

*A fine hill walk with outstanding
views to enjoy.*

| | |
|---|---|
| **DISTANCE** 5 miles (8km) | **MINIMUM TIME** 1hr 30min |
| **ASCENT/GRADIENT** 476ft (145m) ▲▲▲ | **LEVEL OF DIFFICULTY** +++ |
| **PATHS** Field paths and country lanes, 13 stiles | |
| **LANDSCAPE** Rolling hills | |
| **SUGGESTED MAP** OS Explorer 191 Banbury, Bicester & Chipping Norton | |
| **START/FINISH** Grid reference: SP 308394 | |
| **DOG FRIENDLINESS** Under control at all times | |
| **PARKING** Village Hall car park in Lower Brailes – donation to hall funds expected | |
| **PUBLIC TOILETS** None en route | |

In medieval times Brailes was the third-largest town in Warwickshire. Today it comprises a pair of small country villages, happily situated off-route, away from the hustle and bustle of the modern towns and cities.

This fine walk takes you over part of Brailes Hill which, at 761ft (232m), is the second-highest point in Warwickshire. From the pretty village of Upper Brailes you walk into Lower Brailes and can enjoy lovely views as you descend into open countryside. You climb above Sutton Brook and will have a wonderful valley view as you go down to Sutton-under-Brailes.

## The Three Brailes

It is a delight to walk through the old part of Upper Brailes where there are a number of thatched cottages and an ancient earthwork and burial ground called Castle Hill. Following the arrival of the Normans in the 11th century, it was used as the basis for a conventional castle of the motte-and-bailey style. Now it is an excellent vantage point for those who wish to play 'King of the Castle'. From the top of its hill you can see the distinctive marks of a medieval ridge-and-furrow cultivation methods in the surrounding fields.

Lower Brailes is also a dreamy place and, although it has no castle, it does contain the 14th-century Church of St George. With its splendid 120-ft (37m) high tower, it is sometimes a referred to as the 'Cathedral of the Feldon', a potentially baffling claim to fame until you learn that 'Feldon' is an old English word for an area of rich fertile farmland. It is without a doubt one of the finest churches in Warwickshire. Inside you'll find some exquisite illuminated manuscripts. These date from the middle of the 13th century and are the work of William de Brailes and Matthew Paris.

Brailes has attracted its fair share of unusual and interesting characters. Nance Austin gained a reputation as the Brailes witch. Apparently she specialised in levitation and had a familiar in the form of a cat. Richard Davies was a worthy Elizabethan scholar who is remembered in a monument above a tomb of black marble in St George's Church.

Field paths lead you around the slopes of Brailes Hill between these three lovely villages, which reward you for taking time to explore on foot.

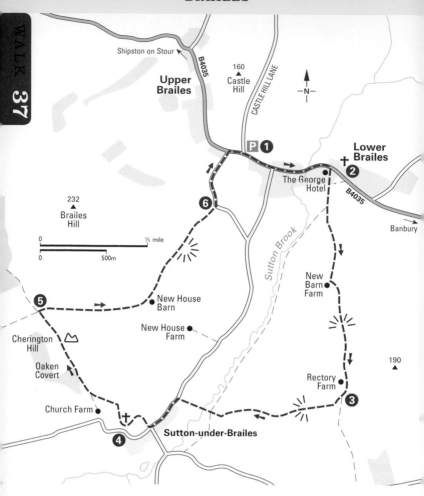

## WALK 37 DIRECTIONS

❶ Leave the car park by the village hall in Lower Brailes to join the B4035. Turn left to stroll up through the beautiful village for about 0.5 mile (800m), first passing the post office and then The George Hotel, which has always been popular with local ramblers (see Where to Eat and Drink).

❷ Turn right and walk down a waymarked public footpath just beyond The George Hotel. This runs beside a small Cotswold dry-stone wall, passing over a low stile, and then through a gate to

cross Cow Lane into pastureland via a stile. Continue ahead and, at a footpath junction waymark post, continue ahead to a double stile and footbridge in the hedge. Over them bear half right to next stile, then a quarter left for two further fields via a stile by a footbridge between them and heading for New Barn Farm. The footpath goes to the left of the farm complex to a stile and you should continue a quarter left up the hill crossing the field to a stile. Cross the corner of the next field and continue ahead on the right-hand side of the hedge – there is a fine retrospective view over Lower Brailes. Walk up the

## WHERE TO EAT AND DRINK

The George Hotel, in the middle of Lower Brailes, has long been a popular eating and drinking place for local walkers and walking groups. Apart from selling fine local ales and excellent home-made food there is a large rear garden to enjoy.

path, then go through a hedge gap and bear right, walking above the trees surrounding the ruinous Rectory Farm.

**3** Bear right at the end of the trees and now begin a gentle descent on a farm track, enjoying a wonderful view ahead over the valley as you proceed towards the village of Sutton-under-Brailes. Pass over a stile, the golf course now to your right, and when you reach the road at the bottom of the hill, turn left and wander through another beautiful Cotswold village, going to the right, past the fine village green, and heading for a stile to the left-hand side of the parish church.

**4** Clamber over the stile, then another, to cross an orchard and walk past the church, then over another stile go half left across the cultivated field by Church Farm on to a farm lane/track via a stile in the far corner. Go right up this track, passing to the right-hand side of Oaken Covert. Continue ahead through a field gate and uphill alongside a post-and-wire fence. Pass through another field gate and, with a hedge on your right, you ascend Cherington Hill.

**5** Just past three pine trees you reach a junction of public footpaths. Go right through a timber bridle gate and follow a tractor track heading generally eastwards. The route goes to the left-hand side of New House

Barn, then veers roughly north-east through a field gate along the top of several farm fields, with more good views over the Brailes Valley to the right. Walk through two fields, passing through a field gate. At end of the second field go through a handgate to descend the hedged track called High Lane, the lower part a deep sunken lane, to reach Tommy's Turn.

## WHILE YOU'RE THERE

Perhaps travel to Tysoe, about 5 miles (8km) north, and explore the lovely village which William the Conqueror gave to one of his followers, Robert de Stafford. In size and importance it ranked, along with Brailes, next to Warwick. From Upper Tysoe you can stroll up to the parish church and enjoy a classic view of the great Tudor mansion of Compton Wynyates – still the seat of the Marquis of Northampton.

**6** Turn left and walk down the lane, continuing your descent into Henbrook Lane. Soon you will come back out on to the High Street in Lower Brailes (the B4035). Turn right along the road for about 100yds (91m) to return to the village hall car park on the corner of Castle Hill Lane.

## WHAT TO LOOK OUT FOR

You will adore the quaint village of Sutton-under-Brailes where time appears to have stood still. Attractive houses surround the picturesque village green and the fine old tombs in the churchyard lie beneath a beautiful spreading chestnut tree. The 13th-century church has a beautiful lofty tower and a 14th- to 15th-century porch. There is a shallow recess on its north side which may once have been a chantry chapel.

# At Hartshill Hayes

*Enjoy fine views from the country park
and along the Coventry Canal.*

---

**DISTANCE** *4.5 miles (7.2km)*   **MINIMUM TIME** *1hr 45min*

**ASCENT/GRADIENT** *295ft (90m)* ▲▲▲   **LEVEL OF DIFFICULTY** ✦✦✦

**PATHS** *Lanes, field paths, woodland tracks and tow paths, no stiles*

**LANDSCAPE** *Country park and rolling countryside*

**SUGGESTED MAP** *OS Explorer 232 Nuneaton & Tamworth*

**START/FINISH** *Grid reference: SP 317943*

**DOG FRIENDLINESS** *Off lead in park and along tow path*

**PARKING** *Hartshill Hayes Country Park, pay and display*

**PUBLIC TOILETS** *Hartshill Hayes Country Park*

---

In 1978, around 136 acres (55ha) of the hillside around Hartshill were made into the fine country park which forms the basis of this walk. It strays into Warwickshire proper and includes part of the Coventry Canal.

It isn't just local people you will meet here enjoying the freedom of this protected countryside and its wide and varied views. Wildlife thrives in the country park too. The spotted flycatcher is also a frequent visitor and, if you are lucky, you may glimpse the low, swooping flight of a sparrow hawk pursuing its prey amid the hedges and woods. A sizeable area of woodland has developed at Hartshill, refreshingly dominated by traditional broadleaved trees such as oak, beech, sycamore, hazel and alder. Elder and holly also thrive.

Hartshill village is an old settlement but there is little information to establish its full history. The Romans were here and may have built a military station on the hill. They would have appreciated the outstanding views which, on a clear day, embrace the faint peaks of Derbyshire.

Hugh de Hardreshull built a motte-and-bailey castle on the hill in 1125. Robert de Hartshill, who became Lord of the Castle, was killed alongside Simon de Montfort at the battle of Evesham in 1265. Perhaps it fell into disuse then, for all traces of the fortification have long since disappeared.

The village's most famous resident was the poet Michael Drayton, a contemporary and friend of William Shakespeare. He was born at the long demolished Chapel Cottage in Hartshill Green in 1563 and there is a plaque in his memory. His poem *A Fine Day* suggests he drew considerable inspiration from the local landscape:

> 'Clear had the day been from the dawn
> All chequered was the sky
> Thin clouds like scarfs of cobweb lawn
> Veiled heaven's most glorious eye.'

In *Polyolbion* he described the River Anker, which weaves its way past his birthplace to join the River Tame, as 'trifling betwixt her banks so slow'.

# HARTSHILL HAYES

## Thriving Canalside Scene

The Coventry Canal came long after Drayton's day. It winds its way along the valley below the village linking Atherstone and the Fazeley Junction, where it joins the main canal system to connect with the Trent and Mersey. The canal reached Fazeley in 1790, happily coinciding with the completion date of the Oxford Canal and allowing it to improve a shaky financial position (under engineer James Brindley its construction had run massively over budget). It remained in a reasonably sound state until 1948 when nationalisation was followed by disuse and deterioration. In recent years, however, it has been successfully restored for pleasure craft to enjoy the pleasing scenery.

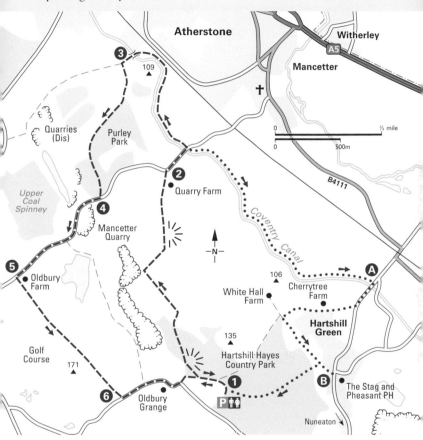

## WALK 38 DIRECTIONS

**1** From the car park enter the Hartshill Hayes Country Park at the back of the visitor centre. Pass the swings and take the path which arcs left (north-west) along the top of Hartshill, alongside a covered reservoir, and enjoy the super view over the surrounding area. Continue ahead across the greensward on the path that then descends gently right into woodland. At the bottom of the woodland go over the two footbridges and then bear left to walk along a fine open path as you continue, initially to the left of the hedge, then to its right. In about 0.25 mile (400m) the path bends to the right and you will ascend north-east to the brow of the hill from where you can overlook the Coventry Canal and get a great view. Bear left beside a kissing gate on to the path which becomes hedged as you progress northwards towards Quarry Farm. Go through the handgate to the left of the farm buildings on to Quarry Lane.

### WHERE TO EAT AND DRINK

The Stag and Pheasant pub in Hartshill is passed on the longer route (Walk 39). It welcomes walkers and allows children in the lounge and on the patio – dogs are allowed in the bar and on the patio. Light refreshment may be obtained from the kiosk at the Hartshill Hayes Country Park visitor centre.

**2** Turn right and stroll down the lane, bearing right at the junction until you come to bridge No 36 over the Coventry Canal. Cross either bridge and descend right to the tow path, go right under the bridge to walk in a north-westerly direction and in 0.5 mile proceed beneath bridge No 37.

**3** Leave the tow path at bridge No 38 and cross the canal on to a quiet lane. Walk up the lane for about 150yds (137m) then, just before a private house, go left through a tall kissing gate into meadowland and on into pastureland. Cross over the

### WHILE YOU'RE THERE

Stroll around Hartshill Green, and note the plaque to the poet Michael Drayton on the side of the block of flats (Drayton Court). Perhaps visit the nearby village of Mancetter – its history embraces Romans, Vikings, Saxons and Normans. You may have seen its church tower from Hartshill Hayes Country Park.

footbridge at the bottom of the field, then walk half right across the next field and on to a gate to a footbridge and a second tall kissing gate and enter the woodland of Purley Park. Follow the footpath up the right edge of the woodland. The path arcs left into the trees and you will exit on to Quarry Lane again.

**4** Go right and head up the lane, past the entrance to Mancetter Quarry. Continue along the lane and in a further 600yds (549m), just past Oldbury Farm, go left.

**5** Walk to the right of the farm buildings with market gardens on your right to reach a good bridlepath beside ponds going south-east. This lovely path crosses arable land, but soon you will be following yellow-topped marker posts across a golf course.

### WHAT TO LOOK OUT FOR

As you return to the country park the walk takes you past Oldbury Grange, now a nursing home, which was built around 1904 by Garside Phillips, the first manager of Ansley Colliery. He bought it for his son Joseph who himself became 'The Boss' at the pit. The Phillips family became the leading gentry in the village. Joseph's grandson is Captain Mark Phillips, the renowned horseman and former husband of Princess Anne.

**6** Exit on to a road, via a handgate, and then go left. The road passes by Oldbury Grange and Adbury Gardens. Where there is a sharp right-hand bend in the road, go left up towards the rear entrance to the gardens and enter Hartshill Hayes Country Park via two gates. Once you are in the park bear right and join the waymarked park path that takes you back to the visitor centre.

# Hartshill Hayes and the Coventry Canal

*An alternative walk through the country park
and along a section of the Coventry Canal.*
**See map and information panel for Walk 38**

> **DISTANCE** *4.5 miles (7.2km)*   **MINIMUM TIME** *2hrs*
> **ASCENT/GRADIENT** *262ft (80m)* ▲▲▲   **LEVEL OF DIFFICULTY** ✦✦✦

## WALK 39 DIRECTIONS (Walk 38 option)

Once over canal bridge No. 36, just after Point ❷, go left (south-east) along the Coventry Canal. As you stroll along there are fine views to the east and up towards Hartshill Hayes Country Park (see Walk 38). Walk along the tow path until you come to bridge No 32 where British Waterways have a maintenance yard on the far bank of the canal and their building has a very interesting clock tower.

Ascend to the road and cross the very narrow canal bridge (Point Ⓐ) with care (there are traffic-lights) and head up the lane towards Hartshill. In 200yds (183m), bear right on to a concrete farm track towards Cherrytree Farm. Follow this track for about 0.5 mile (800m) and then, just before the track bears right to go up to the farm complex, go sharp left through a kissing gate into meadowland.

Bear left and walk along the left edge of the meadow, often amid scrub, and below a row of houses up to the left. In about 0.5 mile (800m) the path arcs left, climbing steeply to a junction of paths situated at the end of the row of flats and houses. You can detour into the village of Hartshill Green to visit the Stag and Pheasant pub (Point Ⓑ).

Return to the footpath and go down the steep steps, crossing a long footbridge and then entering woodland on Hartshill Green. Walk up the waymarked path through the deciduous trees, always staying on the main route. The path arcs generally towards the north-west and eventually you will turn left to emerge from the trees, via a kissing gate, on to the main path in the park. Bear left and return to the visitor centre car park at Point ❶.

# Coventry City Tour

*A short tour of the historic parts of Coventry.*

| | |
|---|---|
| **DISTANCE** 3 miles (4.8km) | **MINIMUM TIME** 1hr 30min |
| **ASCENT/GRADIENT** 16ft (5m) ▲▲▲ | **LEVEL OF DIFFICULTY** +++ |
| **PATHS** Street pavements, no stiles | |
| **LANDSCAPE** Historic Coventry | |
| **SUGGESTED MAP** AA Street by Street: West Midlands | |
| **START/FINISH** Grid reference: SP 335789 | |
| **DOG FRIENDLINESS** On lead at all times | |
| **PARKING** Any park-and-ride car park, then travel into city by bus | |
| **PUBLIC TOILETS** Library Building in Smithford Way | |

## WALK 40 DIRECTIONS

From the tourist information office in the west tower below the great spire of roofless Old St Michael's Cathedral, go out into Cuckoo Lane, then left down Bayley Lane. St Mary's Guildhall, built in the early 14th century and still boasts one of the finest great halls in England, is on the right. At the corner go left (southwards) to reach Earl Street, then left along Earl Street and into Jordan Well.

Cross the road at the pedestrian crossing and head right, down Whitefriars Street. At the bottom of the street, just before the car park, go right along cobbled Whitefriars Lane, passing beneath the Whitefriars Gateway (remains of a Carmelite Friary founded in 1342) into Park Street. Go right along Park Street, then left along St John's Street to Little Park Street, with the police station, probation service offices and the magistrates courts on the corner.

Go right along Little Park Street and then left over the pedestrian crossing in front of the impressive Council House, built between 1913 and 1917 in Tudor style. Head left along the High Street, past the Cathedral Lanes Shopping Centre to the 1949 Lady Godiva statue, by Sir William Reid Dick.

When you have seen the statue, walk back towards the High Street and go right down Greyfriars Lane opposite. Just after you pass by Salt Lane is Ford's Hospital. These wonderful old almshouses were badly damaged by bombing in 1940 but were restored in 1953. Continue along Greyfriars Lane and take the pathway to the right of the impressive 230-ft (70m) Greyfriars Spire, all that remains of the 14th-century Church of Christ Church, to arrive in New Union Street. Go left and soon cross the street to go through the archway, Manor Yard, to see Cheylesmore Manor (the gatehouse is all that remains of the Manor of the Earl of Chester), until you come to Manor House Drive. Go right and just past Quadrant Hall, go right again down a footpath which takes you to Warwick Road. Cross Warwick Road and head right to the shopping precinct at Bull Yard. Here turn left down into Shelton Square. Bear right and continue along Market Way into the centre of the main shopping area.

### WHILE YOU'RE THERE

Visit Coventry's cathedrals. Located close to one another, it is interesting to see the Old Cathedral which was so badly damaged during the Second World War and to compare it with the revolutionary design of the New Cathedral. There's a simply stunning tapestry, by Graham Sutherland, above the altar.

By the central fountain, go left into the Lower Precinct passing by a number of large, high street stores. At the traffic island by St John's Church, cross the road and head down Spon Street, a fascinating street of medieval buildings, to see more of historic Coventry. At the end do not attempt to go over the Ringway but retrace your steps to the traffic island by St John's Church. Go left just before the church and stroll past the buildings of Old Bablake School, which was founded in 1560 for the education of poor boys of Coventry, and into Hill Street. Bear right along Bond Street and left into Corporation Street. Reaching the Coventry Evening Telegraph offices, go left into Upper Well Street, then right into Lamb Street. Turn left at

The Stag to a footbridge over The Ringway that leads to the Canal Basin. The Basin has been carefully renovated and displays a Y-shaped terminus, canal warehouses, coal vaults and a fine canal house.

Retrace your steps over the footbridge and walk down Bishop Street. Go left along Tower Street then right down to Cook Street, turning left alongside the rear of the Coventry Transport Museum. After going beneath 15th-century Cook Street Gateway, turn right and stroll through Lady Herbert's Garden to reach Hales Street by the Swanswell (Priory) Gate. This 15th-century gate was probably a private access into St Mary's Priory. Pass in front of the Coventry Transport Museum which houses the UK's largest display of British-made vehicles and go right along Hales Street until you reach a road junction, then go left up The Burges. Bear left around Ironmonger Row and cross the road. Go right and then left into Priory Row and proceed down between the New and the Old Cathedrals. After visiting the New Cathedral (designed by Sir Basil Spence the then ultra-modern St Michael's Cathedral caused quite a stir when it was consecrated in 1962), cross over into the Old Cathedral which was also devastated by bombs in 1940 and walk through the damaged building up to Cuckoo Lane and back to the tourist information office.

### WHERE TO EAT AND DRINK

There are plenty of places to eat in Coventry. The route of this walk takes you past several of the finest pubs. The Old Windmill and the Shakespeare in Spon Street, the Town Wall Tavern in Bond Street, the Tudor Rose in The Burges and the Golden Cross in Hay Lane.

# On Edge
# at Ratley

*A walk along Edgehill, scene of a major Civil War battle,*
*with a visit to Upton House.*

| | | |
|---|---|---|
| **DISTANCE** 6 miles (9.7km) | | **MINIMUM TIME** 2hrs 15min |
| **ASCENT/GRADIENT** 164ft (50m) ▲▲▲ | | **LEVEL OF DIFFICULTY** +++ |
| **PATHS** Lanes and field paths, 4 stiles | | |
| **LANDSCAPE** Rolling countryside | | |
| **SUGGESTED MAP** OS Explorer 206 Edge Hill & Fenny Compton | | |
| **START/FINISH** Grid reference: SP 362458 | | |
| **DOG FRIENDLINESS** On lead at all times | | |
| **PARKING** On lay-by on A422 | | |
| **PUBLIC TOILETS** None en route | | |

This hilly walk takes you along the escarpment of the famous Edgehill – a prominent sandstone ridge which runs north-east to south-west at a height of around 600ft (183m) above sea level.

## First of Many Battles

Below the ridge, on the land which stretches away towards Kineton, the first major battle of the Civil War took place in October 1642. It pitted the cavaliers of King Charles I against a poorly equipped Parliamentarian army under Robert Devereux, Earl of Essex. Prince Rupert led the charge of the King's cavalry on his galloping white charger, as he would throughout the coming campaign, but on this day the outcome was inconclusive. The fighting petered out when darkness fell, the Royalists hastening back towards Banbury, the Parliamentarians to Warwick. Neither side could claim a victory. Entering the field with some 14,000 men apiece, they departed leaving around 3,000 casualties in total, and lost perhaps as many men again as deserters. You can't visit the actual battle site today, as it is hidden in a huge Ministry of Defence ammunition facility, but an Edgehill Battle Museum can be found in the grounds of Farnborough House, some 3 miles (4.8km) to the east. The splendid Radway Tower, passed towards the end of the walk, was constructed to mark the 100th anniversary of the battle, though it wasn't completed until 1750. This 70ft (21m) octagonal folly is now occupied by the popular Castle Inn.

## Views from the Ridge

There are other monuments and views to be seen from the ridge. From Ratley you can see an obelisk erected in 1854 by Charles Chambers to commemorate the Battle of Waterloo. At Nadbury Camp the mounds of an 18-acre (7ha) Bronze Age camp can still be seen, although the remains have been dissected by a busy road and there has been considerable damage by ploughing. The walk also takes you close to the National Trust's Upton House (see While You're There) before descending into the medieval village of Ratley.

You'll find Ratley is a peaceful village, set away from the main Oxford road and largely unchanged since the turn of the 20th century. Its recognition in

# RATLEY

1971 as a conservation area has helped ensure the survival of its oldest p
Records show the manor was held by a Saxon named Ordic before the arr
of the Normans. Most of its houses are built of honey-brown Hornton stone –
local limestone produced in the Edgehill Quarry. Quarrying was once a majo
local industry. Today the quarried land has been reclaimed, planted with trees
and has become a nature reserve. An active farming community remains, but
most local people commute to Oxford for work.

Ratley's 12th-century church is near the Rose and Crown pub and has the
unusual dedication of St Peter ad Vincula (see What to Look Out For). Outside
it is an ancient preaching cross; time has robbed it of its arms, and only the shaft
remains. As you return to the start, there are views over farmland to Tysoe.

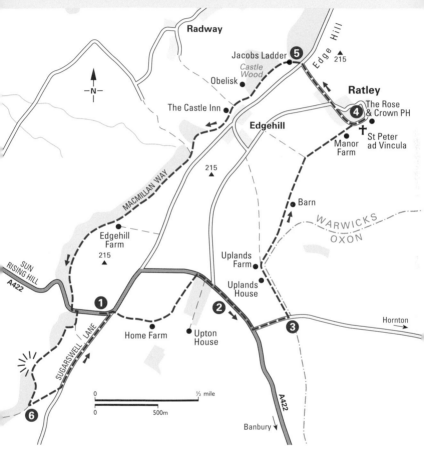

## WALK 41 DIRECTIONS

❶ From the lay-by on the A422 walk east, go left and in 10yds (9m) go right again through a farm gate, following a stone wall, then, through another gate, bear left towards Home Farm. Pass to the left of the farm buildings, then go left and aim for the far right corner of the field and two kissing gates. Continue via a kissing gate through the National Trust car park to another gate and the A422. Go right along the grass verge of the busy road past the entrance gates to the 17th-century Upton House (known for its art collection).

# RATLEY

...about 600yds (549m), cross ...422 with care and go left ...wn the lane to Hornton.

**3** In a further 300yds (274m) go left along a signed path. Walk to the left of the field hedge over two fields, then pass to the right of the buildings of Uplands House and Uplands Farm. Continue through a gate into open countryside bearing right down a track to a farm gate and stile and descend into the valley. Walk by the hedge and pass to the left of an old dilapidated barn and, across a stile, ascend to a junction of paths. Go left through a gate and immediately over a stile to continue ahead, descending a farm field to reach another stile in the far right corner. Go over a stone stile to emerge in Ratley village by Manor Farm.

**4** At the main road go right to explore the old village, then retrace your steps past Manor Farm and continue along the road towards Edgehill.

**5** Cross over the road at the T-junction and descend Jacobs Ladder into Castle Wood opposite, following the waymarkers of the MacMillan Way, ignoring the gate into open countryside. Take the footpath along the escarpment of

the famous hill. After about 0.25 mile (400m) of walking, look right to see the Obelisk, then continue along the escarpment path, passing below the Castle Inn. Walk along the escarpment path, sometimes in the edge of the wood and sometimes with the hedge on your left and trees on your right for about 1.25 miles (2km). Keep on the MacMillan Way until you reach the A422, at the top of Sun Rising Hill. Cross the road and continue along the concrete track, initially bearing right at stables, then left before taking the left path, soon passing through a gate to open land with a superb view of Tysoe and the surrounding countryside. Continue through a second gate and follow a path on the edge of the woods for about 300yds (274m).

**6** Go left through a farm gate and diagonally left across the field to reach Sugarswell Lane via a handgate. Continue left along the lane to the A422 and the lay-by.

# Busy Bedworth and the Canals

*An easy walk to see Hawkesbury Junction*
*where the Coventry and Oxford canals meet.*

---

**DISTANCE** 4.5 miles (7.2km)   **MINIMUM TIME** 1hr 45min

**ASCENT/GRADIENT** 56ft (17m) ▲▲▲   **LEVEL OF DIFFICULTY** +++

**PATHS** Lanes, field paths, woodland tracks and tow paths, 7 stiles

**LANDSCAPE** Canalside and gentle countryside

**SUGGESTED MAP** OS Explorer 221 Coventry & Warwick

**START/FINISH** Grid reference: SP 362839

**DOG FRIENDLINESS** Off lead along tow path, otherwise under control

**PARKING** Near Elephant and Castle in Hawkesbury

**PUBLIC TOILETS** None en route

---

This easy walk gives you the opportunity to share a Midlands canal experience by walking the tow paths of two of the area's most important canals. They formed an important link in Britain's network of canals during the Industrial Revolution.

The route takes you from Hawkesbury through pleasant countryside to reach the Coventry Way. After passing newly constructed Hollybush Lakes fishery, Coalpit Fields Woodlands Nature Reserve and the Mineral Lakes fishery, you join the Coventry Canal near Bedworth. Allthough it is quiet now, this was once a major coalmining community. You'll pass the Hawkesbury Junction conservation area where the elegant 50-ft (15m) Britannia Foundry of Derby's cast-iron bridge, built in 1837, spans the junction of the Coventry and Oxford canals.

## The Coventry and Oxford Canals

Hawkesbury Junction was also known as Sutton Stop, after the name of the first lock keeper. It became a famous resting place for bargees on this part of the canal system. In 1821 an engine house was built to pump water up into the canal from a local well. The Newcomen-type atmospheric steam engine which lifted the well water was called Lady Godiva. It ceased pumping in 1913 and has since been transferred to the Dartmouth Museum in Devon. Thomas Newcomen was born in Dartmouth in 1663, and Lady Godiva forms the centrepiece of his memorial museum. At Hawkesbury Junction, The Greyhound Inn and the pump house are reminders of this once busy scene. Photographers will find a classic shot through the archway of the cast-iron bridge.

## Grand Trunk Objective

The Act of Parliament to enable the construction of the Coventry Canal was passed in 1768 with two objectives. Firstly to connect Coventry with a new trade route called the Grand Trunk (today known as the Trent and Mersey Canal), and secondly to provide Coventry with cheap coal from the coalfield at Bedworth, a major mining community. By 1769 the

...etch of canal between Coventry and Bedworth had been completed but, ...ecause of some wrangling with the Oxford Canal Company, the Coventry Canal did not reach its point of linkage with the Grand Trunk at Fazeley until 1790. James Brindley was the original engineer for this attractive, contour canal, but he was sacked from the job following an overspend of authorised capital.

## Coals to London

Brindley was also the engineer of the winding 91-mile (146km) Oxford Canal, one of the earliest to be built. Its objective was to connect the Midlands with London. It reached Oxford in 1789 and was completed in 1790. Initially the link was achieved with the Coventry Canal via a 1-mile (1.6km) parallel stretch of canal. In 1801 the Hawkesbury Junction was constructed to avoid this costly duplication. The price of coal in the capital, which was previously transported from Newcastle by sea, dropped almost immediately.

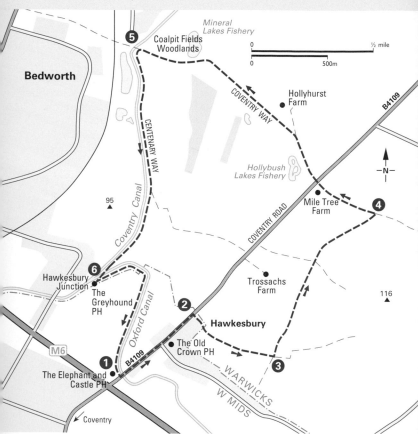

## WALK 42 DIRECTIONS

❶ From the Elephant and Castle ascend to the Coventry Road. Go left, crossing the bridge over the Oxford Canal and follow the road past the Old Crown.

❷ In about 250yds (229m), just before the large sign for Bedworth and Nuneaton, go right and take the footpath into meadowland. Continue along the footpath to a stile, then go left over the stile into a large field. Cross the field, heading towards a double stile at the end, but don't go over the stile.

**WHERE TO EAT AND DRINK**

You are spoilt for choice around Hawkesbury. The Elephant and Castle is by the Oxford Canal in Hawkesbury and welcomes walkers – children and dogs are allowed in the gardens. The walk passes the Old Crown in the village and then at Hawkesbury Junction, The Greyhound. This is attractively placed and has large gardens where children and dogs are allowed.

**WHILE YOU'RE THERE**

Spend a little time at Hawkesbury Junction enjoying the magical scene with its traditionally decorated narrowboats as their occupants visit the chandlery (or The Greyhound) or manoeuvre between the two canals. This once busy industrial canal centre is now used solely for leisure purposes.

merge left with grass track and shortly go over a stile on to a farm track. Follow this track as it arcs left past the Mineral Lakes Fishery sign to reach bridge No 13 over the Coventry Canal.

**3** Go left again and head towards another stile in the field corner. Cross this and continue in a north-easterly direction over two stiles and three kissing gates. Your route passes by Trossachs Farm (on the left) and you continue along the path by the field edge. After going over a stile and footbridge, walk diagonally over a large field, aiming to the left of an ash tree in the far corner.

**5** Just before reaching the bridge, go left and descend to the tow path along the pleasant canal. Head south along the tow path – this is part of the Centenary Way. The path arcs gently right (south-west) and soon you reach Hawkesbury Junction where large numbers of colourful narrowboats are usually moored and The Greyhound pub offers a welcome break.

**4** Go over the stile, then left to join the Coventry Way. Take the track by the field edge until you exit on to the Coventry road once again via a stile, near to Mile Tree Farm. Cross the road to a sign for Hollybush Lakes and continue ahead on a track heading past fishing lakes generally towards Hollyhurst Farm. Follow the Coventry Way as the path arcs left at a waymark post and you go through a hedge gap. Soon, beyond a pair of kissing gates, you pass into an area which is being prepared as a nature reserve – this is called Coalpit Fields Woodlands. Continue ahead through copse and

**WHAT TO LOOK OUT FOR**

The canals are heavily used by local anglers, usually with rods much taller than themselves. You may see pike, roach, perch, bream or carp being hauled on to the bank. If you stroll off the main route at Bedworth Hill Bridge you can visit two small lakes where, apparently, the fish are meant to be even bigger.

**6** Cross the cast-iron footbridge and leave the Coventry Canal, going left along the Oxford Canal tow path. Walk beneath the electricity pylons and make your way back to the Elephant and Castle in Hawkesbury.

# Harbury, Chesterton and the Lakes

*A pleasant walk into typical Warwickshire countryside to visit the lovely church at Chesterton.*

| | |
|---|---|
| **DISTANCE** 4 miles (6.4km) | **MINIMUM TIME** 1hr 45min |
| **ASCENT/GRADIENT** 131ft (40m) ▲▲▲ | **LEVEL OF DIFFICULTY** ✦✦✦ |

**PATHS** Farm driveways and field paths, 3 stiles

**LANDSCAPE** Rolling Warwickshire countryside

**SUGGESTED MAP** OS Explorer 206 Edge Hill & Fenny Compton

**START/FINISH** Grid reference: SP 373597

**DOG FRIENDLINESS** Under control at all times

**PARKING** Village hall car park in Harbury

**PUBLIC TOILETS** None en route

This walk starts from one of the most historic places in Warwickshire, for Harbury was once the home of a huge ichthyosaurus that roamed the local countryside. Its skeleton and those of a plesiosaurus and several marine dinosaurs have been found in the old quarries here, as have Bronze Age cooking pots.

## A Woman's Place

In about 500 BC there was an Iron Age camp (or byrig) in these parts. It was ruled by a woman called Hereburh, and Harbury's name derives from 'the fortified place belonging to a woman called Hereburh'.

The Romans were also here. Their great Fosse Way forms one of the boundaries to the village and Roman culverts can still be seen. Ridge and furrow fields reveal evidence of Saxon farmers, and an area called Temple End suggests the land was once owned by the Knights Templar.

## Minor Poets

The parish church of All Saints is mostly Norman and dates from the 13th century. It sports a sundial carrying the accusatory inscription 'Tyme flyeth, what doest thou?' The Wagstaffes were the 'proprietors' of the manor from the time of Henry VIII (1491–1547) and inside the church is a memorial to Jane Wagstaffe who lived here during Elizabeth I's reign. Behind the church is the Tudor 'Wagstaffe School' which was founded by Jane's descendants in 1611. The vicar from 1746 to 1771 was Richard Jago who was something of a minor poet. Today, Harbury is a delightful old village where you can see attractive cottages, imbibe in fine pubs and admire some lovely old trees.

From Harbury, the walk takes you south along peaceful country lanes passing by attractive lakes to reach the tiny hamlet of Chesterton – a place of rare beauty where time appears to have stood still. The name of the hamlet is of Roman origin. The village was hit very badly by the plague of 1349 and by the 15th century there were only three families residing here. It has recovered a little since then, but much of its former extent has survived for archaeologists to discover (see Walk 44).

*Opposite: St Giles Church, Chesterton (Walk 43).*

### ...cial Church

...day there is no shop or pub in this lovely hamlet, but St Giles' Church is ...ther special. Its embattled parapet runs the entire length of the chancel, ...nd is set on walls which are 3-ft (0.9m) thick. It was founded by Richard the Forester and was presented to the priory at Kenilworth in Richard II's time (1377–99). Sir Edward Peyto built the wonderful landmark four-sail windmill. The return route takes you over pastureland and cultivated fields, passing by an old watermill before reaching Harbury village.

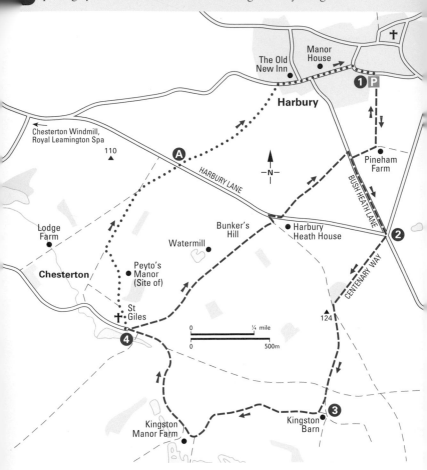

## WALK 43 DIRECTIONS

❶ Leave the car park behind the village hall and head south by football pitches to a gate in the far corner, then follow the waymarkers for the Centenary Way. Continue in a southerly direction to a second gate onto Bush Heath Lane. Turn left and walk down to a junction of lanes.

❷ Go right here, signed 'Kingston Farm' over a cattlegrid and along the grass verge of a driveway for about 600yds (549m), still following the Centenary Way. Where the Way goes off to the left, bear right to continue along a quiet country lane. Soon the buildings of Kingston Barn farm will be to your left, but continue along the lane as it goes to the right of the farm complex until you reach a lane going off to the right.

**3** Proceed right along this lane, which weaves its way through some very attractive countryside. When you reach the garden walls to Kingston Manor Farm, turn right again and continue along the lane, now heading in a north-westerly direction, passing some lovely lakes. After about 0.5 mile (800m) of easy walking past the picturesque lakes, the lane arcs left up towards St Giles' Church in the hamlet of Chesterton. Through a gate or over a cattlegrid, continue up the lane towards the church.

**4** Just before reaching the church gate, go right through a kissing gate and ascend over pastureland and cultivated fields, following the footpaths and heading generally north-east back towards Harbury. The footpath

crosses two stiles and passes to the right of an old windpump and Bunker's Hill. Head towards the left hand of a group of houses, then left along the field edge to a gate on to Harbury Lane, near Harbury Heath House. Turn right and after 100yds (91m), turn left through a kissing gate on a footpath that initially is to the right of the field hedge and later to the left, until you reach Bush Heath Lane. Over a stile turn right on to a lane, then shortly through a gate to rejoin the Centenary Way once again. The path leads towards Pineham Farm. After about 200yds (183m), go left through a gate to return to the car park at the back of Harbury village hall.

# Harbury and Chesterton

*A longer walk to see more of Chesterton and its fine old windmill.*
**See map and information panel for Walk 43**

DISTANCE *5 miles (8km)*   MINIMUM TIME *2hrs 15min*
ASCENT/GRADIENT *180ft (55m)* ▲▲▲   LEVEL OF DIFFICULTY +++

## WALK 44 DIRECTIONS (Walk 43 option)

This short extension to Walk 43 gives you the opportunity to spend time in Chesterton. It is recommended that you get hold of a copy of the leaflet *Discover Chesterton – A Journey Through Time*, produced by the Warwickshire Archaeology Research Team. It provides a map showing the many historic locations around Chesterton.

When you reach Chesterton leave Walk 43 at Point ❹ and pass through the entrance gate to St Giles' Church, taking time to admire this lovely building (see What To Look Out For, Walk 43).

Exit the churchyard through the handgate at its rear, near the chancel. The ornamental Peyto gateway in the north churchyard wall to the left was designed by Inigo Jones and built to provide a suitable entry for the Peyto family when attending church.

Descend the field and go over the footbridge, with a stile at each end, in the hedge below, then over another stile into the next field. Head straight uphill and at the brow aim to the left of some rather derelict buildings.

In the valley to the left are the buildings of Lodge Farm. To the south-west of these are the remains of a medieval settlement, called Netherend in a document of 1319.

Go through the handgate and then right, through a farm gate. A second handgate leads into a large field which you cross going north-east towards a handgate in the fence – the site of the Peyto's manor house is to the right of here.

Through a gate, take the right of two paths, heading to the far right hand corner of a large field, following the waymark direction and, via a gate, exit on to Harbury Lane (Point ❹). Cross the lane, go over a footbridge and through a kissing gate and maintain your direction over several fields, passing through kissing gates, over footbridges and through gates until you emerge through another gate by a house in Temple End in Harbury. Go right along the road and you will pass by the Old New Inn and the Manor House as you progress into Park Lane. Bear right into South Parade, to return to the car park at the rear of the village hall (Point ❶).

From certain positions on this walk Chesterton Windmill comes into view. Unfortunately there are no footpaths to provide a link route to the windmill, however, access is possible from a permissive path off a nearby road.

*Opposite: Chesterton Windmill at sunrise (Walks 43 and 44).*

# Eathorpe and Wappenbury

*A riverside stroll into
the Warwickshire countryside.*

| | |
|---|---|
| **DISTANCE** 3.5 miles (5.7km) | **MINIMUM TIME** 1hr 30mins |
| **ASCENT/GRADIENT** 82ft (25m) ▲▲▲ | **LEVEL OF DIFFICULTY** ✚✚✚ |
| **PATHS** Mainly field footpaths and farm tracks, 7 stiles | |
| **LANDSCAPE** Gentle countryside | |
| **SUGGESTED MAP** OS Explorer 221 Coventry & Warwick | |
| **START/FINISH** Grid reference: SP 392689 | |
| **DOG FRIENDLINESS** Under control at all times | |
| **PARKING** Near The Plough in Eathorpe | |
| **PUBLIC TOILETS** None en route | |

## WALK 45 DIRECTIONS

This is a pleasant stroll through the attractive hidden villages south-east of Coventry. The route starts at Eathorpe, going near to the River Leam over pleasant Warwickshire countryside to the historic village of Wappenbury, then crossing the river to Hunningham before returning to Eathorpe along an unclassified road.

From The Plough, go left down the lane into the village of Eathorpe. The name is derived from 'ea' relating to water and 'thorpe' which is a common Old Norse suffix that

### WHAT TO LOOK OUT FOR

Explore the village of Wappenbury. As well as some idyllic thatched cottages, impressive Wappenbury Hall was once the home of Sir William Lyons, the founder of Jaguar Motors. In the Church of St John the Baptist, see the canopied wall monument of a woman sitting sadly in a harvest field – this is in memory of Thomas Urnbers a patron of 19th-century scientific agriculture.

usually denotes a farmstead. Go right along the main street, walking past the village hall and a lovely pair of thatched cottages called Myrtle and Thyme Cottages. At the end of the village the road bends left and goes over the River Leam.

### WHERE TO EAT AND DRINK

The Plough in Eathorpe is a regular haunt for walking groups. Good food and good ale are the order of the day. At The Red Lion in Hunningham, chicken with cranberry and other delicious home-made foods may appeal. Children are allowed in both pubs, but dogs are restricted to the large gardens.

In 80yds (73m), go right over a stile into pastureland and follow the footpath to the left of the river. After crossing a couple of fields you will come to a fence with a distant view of Princethorpe College with its fine turrets. Aim for the stile in the left corner by a farm gate and follow the waymarker direction (north) until you reach a footbridge over a stream.

Don't cross the footbridge but go sharp left towards the two farm gates in the corner of the field. Go through the metal gate to the left (there is a waymarker on the back of the gatepost) and continue along the farm track to the left of the hedge. Follow this track over several fields via a kissing gate and two field gates until you come to a field gate at the road in the village of Wappenbury, to the right of the walls of Wappenbury Hall's grounds.

Early records show a variety of names for the village but it is likely that it means 'Wappa's fortified place'. It was certainly once fortified and the great earthworks can still be seen here – they are believed to be the largest in the Midlands. During excavations four kilns dating to about AD 350 have been found and a few items of Roman greyware. We have no reason to doubt that the village thrived into the Middle Ages, but then, like so many others in the area, the plague came, taking the lives of some 200 villagers. Wappenbury has never recovered its original size. The Church of St John the Baptist has a 15th-century tower and two coffin lids are the oldest stones in the village. Gravestones and murals make fascinating reading and the mural tablet inside the church reads:

> *'A lingering sickness did me seize*
> *And no physician could me ease*
> *I fought for help but all in vain*
> *Until the Lord did ease my pain.'*

Turn left along the village road until you come to the front gates of Wappenbury Hall. Go right here towards the Church of St John the Baptist – to its left you will see a fine thatched cottage called Garden Cottage. Walk along the lane to the right of the church and continue right, by a laurel hedge, passing to the right of a country cottage. Head back into the open countryside. Go left at a footpath fork through a gate on to a footpath descending to a gate on to a stone and concrete footbridge. After about 0.5 mile (800m) of easy walking and passing through two gates, you will come to the road in the village of Hunningham via a gate. To visit The Red Lion pub turn right through the village for about 0.25 mile (400m).

## WHILE YOU'RE THERE

Just 4 miles (6.4km) to the north of Eathorpe is the 100-acre (40ha) Ryton Pools Country Park. It's a fine place to spot water birds – look especially for great crested grebes, swans, moorhens and Canada geese on the 10-acre (4ha) Ryton Pool. Pagets Pool attracts dragonflies and there are often 17 species around the lake. Look out for the common blue and emperor dragonfly and the black-tailed skimmer.

If you do not visit the pub, go left and walk up the farm drive towards Hunningham Farm, signed Leam Lodge and Unclassified County Road. Continue between the farm buildings, the road now no more than a good stone farm track. After following this road for about 600yds (549m), you will see that it bends to the right about 80 paces ahead of you. Look out for a stile here, leading on to a footpath going off to the left towards the River Leam once again. Walk along the footpath close to the river bank once again. From the river the footpath veers right over three stiles until you come back to the road on the edge of Eathorpe. Go left along the road, passing the entrance to Eathorpe Hall and its fine lodge to return to the village. Turn right up the lane and back to The Plough.

# All Sorts of Dassetts

*A Burton Dassett Hills walk into
Fenny Compton and Farnborough.*

| | |
|---|---|
| **DISTANCE** 7.25 miles (11.7km) | **MINIMUM TIME** 3hrs |
| **ASCENT/GRADIENT** 656ft (200m) ▲▲▲ | **LEVEL OF DIFFICULTY** +++ |

**PATHS** Field paths and farm tracks, 22 stiles

**LANDSCAPE** Hilly countryside

**SUGGESTED MAP** OS Explorer 206 Edge Hill & Fenny Compton

**START/FINISH** Grid reference: SP 394523

**DOG FRIENDLINESS** Under control at all times

**PARKING** Burton Dassett Hills Country Park car park – small charge

**PUBLIC TOILETS** At car park

This lovely walk takes you from the very top of the Dassett Hills in the Burton Dassett Hills Country Park and through the nearby hamlets and villages of Northend, Fenny Compton, Farnborough, Avon Dassett and Burton Dassett. It's the nearest you will get in Warwickshire to wild country, with its bare hills reminiscent of the Peak District. The 100-acre (40ha) country park was opened in 1971, and is set high above the noisy M40 motorway, which didn't arrive until a couple of decades later. It comprises a dramatic mix of rugged, grassy humps and hills with a quaint, small beacon perched on the highest point, actually the tower of a former windmill. There are a number of quarries around the side of the hills which may date back as far as the Iron Age. Today they are covered in grass and offer welcome shelter for picnicking visitors. The view from the top of the hills is quite outstanding.

## A Watering Hole or Two

Initially the walk descends into Northend hamlet then field paths lead you into the village of Fenny Compton. Fenny is an unusual, but not infrequent, prefix in the Midlands and indicates the presence of wetland. The village lies below the Dassett Hills, which give rise to at least seven springs. It was to harness these, to supply around 40 consumers in the village, that one of England's smallest water supply companies was established in 1866.

You pass by several very attractive cottages to reach the impressive Church of St Peter and St Clare – only two churches in England carry this unusual dedication.

The walk continues over Windmill Hill offering fine views over the surrounding countryside. You then descend into the village of Farnborough and find more old stone cottages and The Inn (Where to Eat and Drink).

After the village of Avon Dassett, the walk then ascends into Burton Dassett, passing by the tiny 12th-century Norman All Saints Church. The hills of the Burton Dassett Hills Country Park have been a constant theme throughout this walk and you finish with a flourish on the last of them, Magpie Hill, to enjoy the fine views.

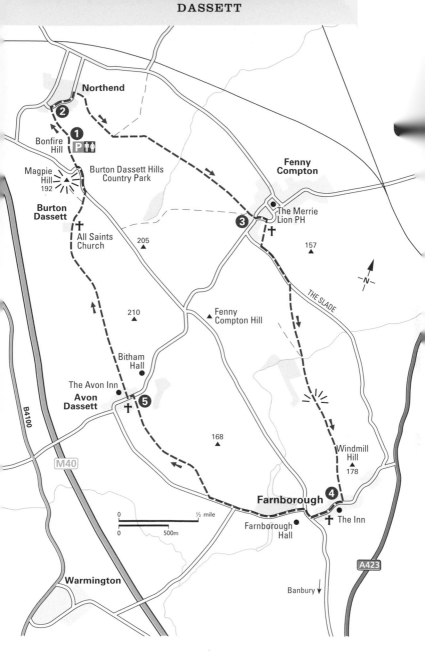

## WALK 46 DIRECTIONS

**❶** From the car park in the Burton Dassett Hills Country Park descend the footpath to the right of Bonfire Hill to a kissing gate onto a track into the village of Northend.

**❷** Go right along Malthouse Lane, soon becoming Top Street, in the village for 300yds (274m), then right again just past Pype Hayes house on to a track between gardens. Then, through a kissing gate, follow the footpath heading generally eastwards towards Fenny

Compton, crossing a mixture of pastureland and cultivated fields via two kissing gates, three stiles and a footbridge, taking your direction from the waymark arrows.

❸ Enter Fenny Compton over a stile, then pass along a hedged path to Grant's Close and go left into Avon Dassett road. Turn right into Dog Lane and go past Duckett Cottage and through the handgate to the right of the village church. Now bear right and cross over pastureland to a gate in the hedge, on to a road known as The Slade. Go left along the road past a large farm barn, then right over a footbridge and through a kissing gate into a large cultivated field. Go half left and follow the footpath signs to cross this field to a second footbridge. Walk up the next field, aiming for a solitary oak in the hedge ahead. Here go left, walk along the field edge and

cross the next field – from the top of the hill there is a fine view of the landmark four-sail windmill at Chesterton (see Walk 43) and the Post Office Communication towers near Daventry. Continue alongside the hedge, follow the direction of the waymarkers, climb Windmill Hill, then descend over farm fields and a hedged footpath into the village of Farnborough, emerging on the main street near the former Butchers Arms, now The Inn.

❹ Head right, along the main street, and bear right past the entrance gates to the National Trust's Farnborough Hall. Continue up the road to the left, past the lake walking along the well-used footpath inside the trees. At the end of the woodland, continue along the road for about 500yds (457m), then go right over a stile and across a couple of cultivated fields into pastureland. Descend to the left of a large barn which brings you to Avon Dassett.

❺ Go left past the Roman Catholic church and in 75yds (69m) go right up a track to the right of The Avon pub into open countryside. Up to the right is the Bitham Hall. The waymarked footpath hugs the top of fields until you arrive in Burton Dassett, passing by its church. Through the kissing gate from the churchyard, continue up the road to the car park near the Beacon.

# Draycote Water, Dunchurch and Thurlaston

*An easy walk around Warwickshire's largest reservoir and into two historic villages.*

| | |
|---|---|
| **DISTANCE** 7 miles (11.3km) | **MINIMUM TIME** 2hrs 30min |
| **ASCENT/GRADIENT** 164ft (50m) ▲▲▲ | **LEVEL OF DIFFICULTY** +++ |

**PATHS** Reservoir paths and field paths, one stile

**LANDSCAPE** Reservoir in gentle rolling countryside

**SUGGESTED MAP** OS Explorer 222 Rugby & Daventry

**START/FINISH** Grid reference: SP 466691

**DOG FRIENDLINESS** Dogs not permitted around the perimeter of Draycote Water

**PARKING** Pay-and-display car park at Draycote Water

**PUBLIC TOILETS** At country park

This walk offers the opportunity to explore the largest area of open water in Warwickshire and to visit two nearby historic villages. The impressive Draycote Water reservoir is set in more than 600 acres (243ha) of land and attracts large numbers of wildfowl. Owned by Severn Trent Water, it was completed in 1970 as a pumped storage facility. It's refilled during winter months from the nearby River Leam, thus reducing the risk of local flooding. There is a fine retrospective view of Draycote Water on your way to lovely Dunchurch village.

## Gunpowder Plot and Treason

A private house in Dunchurch is now called Guy Fawkes but was formerly the Falcon Inn. It was here that the gunpowder plot conspirators sought refuge from justice in 1605, after their failed attempt to assassinate King James I as he visited parliament. Dunchurch was once a busy coaching village and the Dun Cow is the old coaching inn, conveniently situated at the village crossroads. The historical perspective continues on the village green, where you will see the old stocks and an ancient cross. By the crossroads is a statue commemorating Lord John Scott, a local landowner and sportsman who, at the time of his death, had recently equipped a new boat to investigate some of the problems of deep-sea fishing.

The 14th-century St Peter's Church has a fine tower, a Norman door and a Norman font. Set inside folding doors is a monument to Thomas Newcombe who was 'a printer to three kings' and founded the 17th-century almshouses. These now add an air of old world charm to the hotchpotch of thatched properties in this pleasant village, which is full of floral colour in the spring and summer.

There's another fine view over the reservoir as you descend into the next village – Thurlaston. Again, a number of attractive thatched cottages catch your eye as you enter, and you pass near to a sail-less windmill (now converted into a private residence). One intriguing road name here is Pudding Bag Lane. The Church of St Edmund was completed in 1848, ally to house the village school. The site was donated by Lord John (he of the statue by the crossroads). The building was used as a church Sundays, but accommodation for the schoolmaster was built into the tower. The present bell tower was added later, but the schoolmaster's accommodation remains as a private residence. Bizarrely the bell rope still passes through one of its rooms.

## WALK 47 DIRECTIONS

**❶** From Draycote Water car park proceed up to the reservoir via a handgate, which is signed Visitor Centre, and then bear to the right following the tarmac lane along the top of Farnborough Dam wall to reach the part of the Water known as Toft Bay.

**2** At the end of Toft Bay, go right and leave the reservoir grounds via a handgate where the lane goes sharp left. Continue ahead for 50 paces, then go right to a handgate and follow the waymarker signs to a footpath that climbs past alpaca pens up towards Toft House. Over a stile, continue ahead along the hedged footpath to the left of modern cartsheds. This bends left on to a lane where you go right up to the A426 Rugby to Dunchurch road. Go left along the road, cross the road bridge and enter the village of Dunchurch, passing a number of attractive thatched properties. The Village Square and St Peter's Church are to the right of the crossroads, with the Dun Cow, an old coaching inn full of character, immediately opposite.

### WHILE YOU'RE THERE
Explore Dunchurch village. It once had some 27 alehouses but now has only two pubs. The stocks remain, but sadly the old gaol was pulled down in 1972. The last person to be held in the gaol was a Peter Murcott who spent his night there supping ale through a straw from a barrel outside the window.

**3** At the crossroads, go left along the pavement of the B4429 past the Dunchurch Social Club. Bear left along School Street and follow the footpath past more thatched properties and the infant school down to the Dunchurch Scout Group Hall. Here, go right and then left along a footpath to the right of the playing fields. Through a kissing gate continue alongside a hedge, through a gate, and proceed over a lane and to the rig. Ryefield Farm via two kiss gates. Go ahead over pastur crossing another lane via two kissing gates, then pass beneath M45 road bridge via two kissing gates before diagonally crossing the next field to a kissing gate and a handgate to enter Thurlaston.

**4** Go to the left by St Edmund's Church and via a gate down a concrete farm track to a kissing gate and a footbridge to enter the perimeter of Draycote Water.

**5** Go right along the walkway by the side of the reservoir around Biggin Bay. To your right Thurlaston Grange can be seen and then you will pass a golf course. Continue around the end of the reservoir, passing by the treatment works, and then stroll along Draycote Bank. To your right is the spire of Bourton-on-Dunsmore church about a mile (1.6km) away; to its right is Bourton Hall. After passing by a picnic area and just before reaching the yachting area, go right through a kissing gate on to a footpath that leads up on to Hensborough Hill. Meander past the trig point, some 371ft (113m) above sea level, and return to the car park via a kissing gate.

### WHERE TO EAT AND DRINK
There are a couple of pubs in Dunchurch. The Green Man is situated along the B4429 Daventry Road. The Dun Cow at the crossroads is a popular eating place for local walkers and welcomes children but not dogs (except guide dogs).

### WHAT TO LOOK OUT FOR
St Peter's Church and Bourton Hall are local landmarks to the west of Draycote Water and are clearly visible as you walk around the beautiful reservoir. Situated on Dunsmore Heath in the village of Bourton-on-Dunsmore, St Peter's has a fine 13th-century font, a Jacobean altar and a ghost in its vestry. The 18th-century Bourton Hall was restored in 1979.

# Sails and Ghosts at Napton on the Hill

*A short hilly walk passing by a famous windmill landmark, visible for much of the route.*

| | |
|---|---|
| **DISTANCE** 2.5 miles (4km) | **MINIMUM TIME** 1hr 15min |
| **ASCENT/GRADIENT** 213ft (65m) ▲▲▲ | **LEVEL OF DIFFICULTY** +++ |

**PATHS** Field paths, farm tracks and country lanes, 3 stiles

**LANDSCAPE** Rolling Warwickshire countryside

**SUGGESTED MAP** OS Explorers 206 Edge Hill & Fenny Compton; 222 Rugby & Daventry

**START/FINISH** Grid reference: SP 463612 (on Explorer 222)

**DOG FRIENDLINESS** Off lead along tow path, otherwise under control

**PARKING** St Lawrence Church car park, Napton on the Hill

**PUBLIC TOILETS** None en route

This walk takes you over Napton Hill and past its historic windmill with its unmoving arms outstretched against the skyline. On a good day you can see seven counties from the windswept summit. Apparently, during the Second World War, the locals sat at the top of the hill to watch the bombing of Coventry and its surrounding area.

## Mill on the Hill

There has been a windmill at Napton on the Hill since 1543 – it is one of the great landmarks in Warwickshire. Next to the privately owned mill building is the former miller's stone cottage, which still houses parts of the original bread oven. Early maps of the area reveal that there were once two windmills on the hill. They drew a regular and pure supply of water from underground springs and wells. The present windmill is in fine condition but not open to the public.

## Industrial Revolution

The village of Napton on the Hill, whose name derives from the old British word Cnapton, meaning 'farm on the knap of the hill', was a substantial settlement in 1086. It was granted a charter in 1321 to hold a weekly market and an annual fair and became a prosperous medieval village. Today, attractive mellowed brown and gold thatched houses contribute to a picturesque scene.

You could be forgiven for thinking this was a timeless image, untouched by the revolutionary industrial changes which were taking place elsewhere in the West Midlands, but even Napton succumbed to 'canal mania' towards the end of the 18th century. Britain was gripped as the whole country clamoured to invest in the new transport technology. In a two-year period in the 1790s, 37 separate Acts of Parliament were passed to enable the construction of an amazing system of 4,250 miles (6,840km) of navigable rivers and canals. The Oxford Canal, completed in 1790, was part of this and it encouraged canalside businesses to develop. Workmen

were more than happy to take alcohol at The Folly Inn while th_
in the construction of the flight of seven Napton Locks.

## A Very Peculiar Church

The 12th-century landmark of St Lawrence's Church, on the brow
hill, is surrounded by a fascinating legend. Originally the church was g
to be built at the bottom of the hill and the stone was assembled ready
its erection. Overnight, however, the stone was mysteriously moved to th_
present site, near the top of the hill and the church was erected where it lay.
The builders obviously decided to construct it where the spirits dictated!
Its dominant position near to the fine windmill is said to be a reminder that
man lives 'under the shadow of the Almighty', but wherever you are on this
walk, the windmill at Napton on the Hill is never far away.

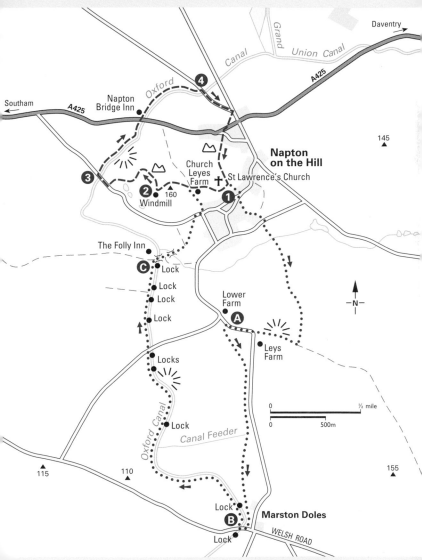

## DIRECTIONS

the car park, walk around
...de of the churchyard of St
...ce's Church and pass by a
...er car park. From here take
...track that becomes a lane and
...ss by Church Leyes Farm. At the
...ane junction, go ahead and follow
the driveway towards the superb
windmill which comes into view –
the building and its land are private
so please respect the 'Private' signs
and keep off the property.

❷ At the entrance by the 'Private'
sign, go right, along a footpath
around the outside of the property,
following the waymarkers.
Through a gate this leads to lovely
open land and you now can go
downhill to follow the path that
arcs right along the fence line.
After crossing a stile, the path
bends sharp left and leads you
towards some delightful fishing
pools. Keep by the fence and you
will soon go through a kissing gate
by the side of Tilehurst house onto
Brickyard Lane. Go right down the

### WHERE TO EAT AND DRINK

The walk route passes two
public houses which welcome
walkers. The Bridge at Napton
is situated on the A425 as
you reach the Oxford Canal.
It offers good food to eat in
its fine canalside gardens. The
Folly Inn (Folly 'Pie Pub') serves
traditional food in its excellent
gardens. It stands by Napton
Bottom Lock and is filled with
charming bygones.

lane and cross bridge No 112 over
the Oxford Canal.

❸ Over the bridge, descend right
on to the tow path, and then walk
to the left. This is easy, pleasant
walking with great views up to
your right of Napton Hill with its
windmill on top.

❹ Leave the tow path at bridge
No 110 via a gate and walk up the
lane back towards the village. At
the road junction with Butt Hill,
go right over a stile and cross
the corner of a field to a further
stile on to the A425 road. Bear
right and cross the main road and
a road called Hillside, then go
through a waymarked handgate and
begin to climb the hill up a clear
hedged footpath. As you approach
the top of the hill, the path
becomes less steep and you will
go through three metal kissing
gates to reach open land once
again. To your right you will see
St Lawrence's Church. Go right
along the church lane back to your
car to complete the walk.

### WHAT TO LOOK OUT FOR

Visit St Lawrence's Church
whose squat tower has, like the
windmill, withstood centuries
of buffeting from the wind.
The north door is called the
Devil's Door and used to be
opened during baptisms for the
Devil to escape. At Christmas
or other festivals you may
hear the ringing of hand bells.
Inside there is a slate portrait
of John Shuckburgh of nearby
Shuckburgh Hall.

### WHILE YOU'RE THERE

A visit to the Nickelodeon Museum is an amazing experience. It once
occupied the old Methodist chapel in Napton, but the number of organs
grew too large and it has been moved to Ashorne Hall, about 12 miles
(19.3km) to the west of here. It's a remarkable working collection of vintage
juke-boxes, symphoniums and many other exotic musical machines. A 1930
replica cinema shows authentic early films. People travel from all over the
country for an evening meal and to recall musical memories of the past.

# To the
# Oxford Canal

*This longer walk includes a stroll along the Oxford Canal.*
**See map and information panel for Walk 48**

**DISTANCE** *6.5 miles (10.4km)* **MINIMUM TIME** *2hrs*
**ASCENT/GRADIENT** *427ft (130m)* ▲▲▲ **LEVEL OF DIFFICULTY** ✚✚✚

## WALK 49 DIRECTIONS
## (Walk 48 option)

From Napton on the Hill this walk ventures into attractive open countryside offering fine views. The route includes a longer stretch of tow path walking along the Oxford Canal, passing by several lock gates and giving the opportunity to visit the Folly Inn.

Cross over the lane at Point **❶** and proceed on the path ahead, descending to Vicarage Road. Head right along the main road for 50yds (46m), then go left down Godsons Lane into Dogs Lane. Go right for 50yds (46m), then left along a hedged bridleway going generally south-east away from Napton.

Continue in this direction for about 350yds (320m), then ahead passing through a series of farm gates. After the third one, go left alongside the hedge, through another field gate, then right alongside a hedge. After two more gates, go right (enjoy the fine retrospective view of Napton on the Hill) to reach a final farm gate to the right of farm buildings – Leys Farm is further to the left. Go along the road, passing Lower Farm (Point **❹**). Just before reaching the junction of roads, go left over a stile and follow the waymarkers as you cross the field diagonally left, going south-east. In the next field head for a stile in a wire fence, then continue to a stile in the hedge ahead and walk parallel with the road hedge, going southwards. Continue over several fields and two stiles, passing to the left of a canal feeder and a derelict building, then cross meadowland until you come to Welsh Road, via a gate, near to Marston Doles (Point **❸**).

Cross canal bridge No 119 and go left, via a gate, to the tow path and turn left under a bridge. Walk along the tow path of the Oxford Canal, heading north towards Napton. Continue past the lock gates. Just after going beneath bridge No 116, there is an exceptional view of Napton. Continue along the tow path to bridge No 113 where you can visit The Folly Inn (Point **❸**).

Cross the bridge into Folly Lane. In 30yds (27m), go left over a stile/footbridge and continue over meadowland and a second footbridge, then proceed along a short stretch of track to a stile. Follow the direction of the waymarker to another stile and cross the large field diagonally to a final stile on to Poplar Road. Go right along the road for 80yds (73m), then left up Hollow Way Lane. This leads back to the lane junction close to Church Leyes Farm. At the junction, go right and return to the car park at St Lawrence's Church (Point **❶**).

# Harborough Magna

*An easy walk through rural villages
and along part of the Oxford Canal.*

---

**DISTANCE** 3.5 miles (5.7km)   **MINIMUM TIME** 1hr 30min

**ASCENT/GRADIENT** 49ft (15m) ▲▲▲   **LEVEL OF DIFFICULTY** ✦✦✦

**PATHS** Field footpaths and tow path, 5 stiles

**LANDSCAPE** Gentle countryside

**SUGGESTED MAP** OS Explorer 222 Rugby & Daventry

**START/FINISH** Grid reference: SP 478792

**DOG FRIENDLINESS** Off lead along tow path, otherwise under control

**PARKING** Village streets near Old Lion pub or, with permission, the pub car park

**PUBLIC TOILETS** None en route

---

## WALK 50 DIRECTIONS

Situated some 4 miles (6.4km) north of Rugby, Harborough Magna is an old village which embraces the hamlets of Harborough Parva and Cathiron. The name Harborough appears to derive from the Saxon English 'heord beorg' meaning 'the hill where flocks are kept'. Its Latinised suffix Magna (Great) was added to distinguish the village from similarly named settlements near by (Parva means Little, in this context).

There was a priest and a mill here when William I's Domesday surveyors entered the parish in their records. Much later, the village also boasted a smithy and a wheelwright, where carts were constructed and repaired for use at the timber yards of William Iven. The whole area seems to have been involved in this industry at some time. Saw mills were located at Cathiron near to the Oxford Canal and the timber was transported via cart and canal barge to the saw mills. Plenty of cart horses were kept locally and teams of horses could be seen hauling the larger trees from the nearby estates to Rugby Station where they were trimmed and cut in readiness for transportation to the saw mills at Cathiron. Sadly this business has now disappeared. With the demise of the industrial use of the canals, pleasure boats now use the Oxford Canal and rambling around the delightful local lanes is a popular pastime for walkers.

This walk starts from the Old Lion pub in Harborough Magna and crosses farmland into the village of Easenhall, which comprises a small number of houses, the 17th-century Golden Lion pub and a couple of farms. Further pastureland is walked on the way to the Oxford

---

### WHAT TO LOOK OUT FOR

If you intend walking around the lanes of Easenhall after dark, look out for the Phantom Horseman. He is apparently the ghost of a one-handed man called Broughton who died in the Old Lawford Hall. Legend has it that, in an attempt to exorcise his ghost, his remains were placed in a phial and tossed into a nearby pond.

Canal. From here a short stretch of tow path leads to more farmland walking on the return journey to Harborough Magna.

> ### WHERE TO EAT AND DRINK
> The walk starts from the car park at the Old Lion in Harborough Magna, which is a popular venue for local walkers. In the village of Easenhall you will pass near the attractive 17th-century Golden Lion with its part wattle-and-daub walls.

From the car park of the Old Lion, cross the B4112 and head up the Main Street opposite into the village. Walk past All Saints Church, noting its unique clock face and continue to the end of the village.

A few paces after passing by Holly Cottage, go right over a stile and follow the footpath across cultivated fields towards the village of Easenhall, climbing another stile. Go over a footbridge to reach the village, via another stile, near an attractive thatched cottage 'Campbell's Cottage'. Go left through the village down to a junction of roads by the village green with the building of the former chapel facing you. The Golden Lion public house is to the right-hand side and to the left you may notice a painted weatherboarded Essex-style house called Brooklands.

Easenhall is a quaint old village of cottages and semi-detached Victorian houses. In the past these were used to accommodate workers of the Manor House at Newbold Revel. The route passes next to the old chapel – a small one-room former Congregational building, now the village hall.

Cross the road and proceed up a hedged footpath to the right of

The Chapel House and after negotiating a handgate and a kissing gate, you will come to open countryside. Continue in a south-westerly direction and through a kissing gate following a path heading towards a prominent footbridge over the main line railway. Go over the footbridge and walk over the next field, crossing bridge No 37, via a kissing gate of the Oxford Canal, and through another kissing gate, arriving on a lane, via a gate.

Go left along the lane for about 600yds (549m) until you come to bridge No 41, where there is an easy descent via steps on to the tow path of this peaceful canal. Go right along the tow path, past Cathiron Farm (on the far bank) and then, at bridge No 43 (Tuckey's Bridge), ascend on to a lane. Cross the bridge and go left to a lane junction and then left again. In 160yds (146m), go right through a handgate and follow the drive going northwards towards Tuckey's Farm. Go through the gate on the right halfway up the drive and head to another to the right of the farm complex. Continue over the next field and through a kissing gate in the hedge, aiming towards houses. Leave the field via a kissing gate and footbridge on to the Easenhall Road with Lodge Farm on your left.

Go right along the road, passing a row of houses. When you are opposite the Cathiron Road junction, go left and take the hedged footpath. Through a kissing gate, briefly follow the hedge and then head diagonally to the far corner of the field, aiming towards a gate. Ignore the gate and cross the next field to a kissing gate by a grey house, bringing you back to Main Street in Harborough Magna. Go right along Main Street, then cross the B4112 to the Old Lion.

# Walking in Safety

All these walks are suitable for any reasonably fit person,
but less experienced walkers should try the easier walks first.
Route finding is usually straightforward, but you will find that
an Ordnance Survey map is a useful addition to the route maps
and descriptions.

## RISKS

Although each walk here has been researched with a view to
minimising the risks to the walkers who follow its route, no walk in
the countryside can be considered to be completely free from risk.
Walking in the outdoors will always require a degree of common
sense and judgement to ensure that it is as safe as possible.

- Be particularly careful on cliff paths and in upland terrain,
  where the consequences of a slip can be very serious.

- Remember to check tidal conditions before walking on the
  seashore.

- Some sections of route are by, or cross, busy roads. Take care
  and remember traffic is a danger even on minor country lanes.

- Be careful around farmyard machinery and livestock, especially
  if you have children with you.

- Be aware of the consequences of changes in the weather and
  check the forecast before you set out. Carry spare clothing and
  a torch if you are walking in the winter months. Remember the
  weather can change very quickly at any time of the year, and
  in moorland and heathland areas, mist and fog can make route
  finding much harder. Don't set out in these conditions unless
  you are confident of your navigation skills in poor visibility. In
  summer remember to take account of the heat and sun; wear a
  hat and carry spare water.

- On walks away from centres of population you should carry a
  whistle and survival bag. If you do have an accident requiring the
  emergency services, make a note of your position as accurately
  as possible and dial 999.

## COUNTRYSIDE CODE

- Be safe, plan ahead and follow any signs.

- Leave gates and property as you find them.

- Protect plants and animals and take your litter home.

- Keep dogs under close control.

- Consider other people.

For more information visit www.countrysideaccess.gov.uk/things_
to_know/countryside_code